SUCCESSFUL LIVING *in a* CHANGING WORLD

EARL NIGHTINGALE

Published and Distributed by
SOUND WISDOM
PO Box 310
Shippensburg, PA 17257-0310
717-530-2122
info@soundwisdom.com
www.soundwisdom.com

Includes content previously published as *This Is Earl Nightingale*.

Curation by Jennifer Janechek
Jacket design by Eileen Rockwell
Text design by Susan Ramundo

ISBN 13: 978-1-64095-116-7
ISBN 13 eBook: 978-1-64095-117-4

For Worldwide Distribution, Printed in the U.S.A.
4 5 6 / 24 23 22 21

CONTENTS

PREFACE

"Human beings rebel against anything simple," says Earl Nightingale. "It seems that in order to be properly impressed, people have to complicate things. We forget what the great teachers have told us; we forget to keep it simple."

Simple, no-nonsense, friendly advice on the art of successful living—that is Nightingale's trademark offering. Raised during the Great Depression, Nightingale was from a young age invested in the pursuit of knowledge, keenly desiring to understand what enabled some people, especially those born without special privileges, to reach their goals while others did not. He dedicated his life to studying success—what it entailed and how to obtain it—and became in the process one of the leading authorities on what makes people successful. The answer?

Success is the progressive realization
of a worthy ideal.

After serving in the Marine Corps, Nightingale built a career in network radio, hosting his own daily commentary program on WGN. Despite making enough money from commission on the program's advertising sales that he could have retired at the age of 35, he decided to purchase an insurance company, spending a significant amount of time motivating its sales force to achieve greatness. Because of his effectiveness in encouraging his employees, one of his sales managers suggested that he record his advice—an idea that resulted in *The Strangest Secret*, the first spoken word message to win a Gold Record by selling over a million copies. Then, in 1960, together with Lloyd Conant, he co-founded Nightingale-Conant, an electronic publishing company that became a world leader in personal development. Nightingale and Conant also worked together to produce a daily radio program called *Our Changing World*, which became one of the longest-running, most widely syndicated radio shows in history.

Successful Living in a Changing World collects the best of Nightingale's ruminations on and recommendations for how to enjoy more of the good things in life. The messages have been curated and edited to reflect modern usage, such as mostly doing away with the generic masculine pronoun that was standard in his time, so that contemporary readers will resonate more strongly with his prose. With his signature wit and wisdom, Nightingale shares in these themes enduring principles that are the bedrock of success in a world that is continuously in flux. Thanks to the extensive reading and study that Nightingale performed during his lifetime, we are now the beneficiaries of timeless truths about achievement, happiness, relationships, personal finance, business, and much more. As we encounter these truths, we can access untapped reservoirs of power deep within us and use them to drive our self-actualization as individuals.

So often, we take for granted everything that life has to offer us and that could be ours, if only we would enlarge our field of vision and take the initiative to act on opportunity. In this collection of messages, Nightingale probes the depths of human psychology and allows no weakness to go unremarked: our tempers, our complacency, our procrastination, and our constant surrender to a sense of inferiority are all held up to the magnifying glass of his microphone and taken to task. Reading these reflections takes us on what Nightingale calls the most profound and interesting journey of our lives—that of self-discovery. It is like having an intimate conversation with a close friend that is simultaneously challenging and invigorating: we might have known all along what we needed to do but would not heed our internal call to action, or perhaps we were ignorant all along of our folly, but regardless—after engaging with Nightingale's words, we are left with the firm sense that we have an exceptional purpose in life and will gain emotional and material success if we direct our mental resources and energy toward its pursuit.

But just because these messages inspire personal reflection does not mean that they are best read in isolation. In fact, readers will discover additional benefits from forming a book club or, if already a member of one, adding this title to their queue. The messages have been categorized thematically so that it is easy to flip through the book and identify and coordinate focus sessions on specific subjects—everything from time management, to creative thinking, to friendships, to additional topics crucial for people who want to make the most of their time on earth. By reading and discussing the selections together, individuals will derive insight from both Nightingale's perspective and the ideas that emerge from others in the group.

However you process these messages, never forget that overcomplication is the gateway to mediocrity. The most enduring truths in the universe are, at their core, the simplest ones—the ones that give us momentum in their clarity and authenticity. Start with this one, found in Nightingale's message of the same title as his most famous radio program:

> *Learn! Learn all you can and keep learning,*
> *whether you are 16 or 60, and you will find your way—*
> *a way infinitely more interesting and substantially more*
> *rewarding—in this changing world of ours.*

FOREWORD

Strange and wonderful things have happened to me with marvelous regularity for as long as I can remember. People and events of various sorts are forever coming along at exactly the right time to help me move from one interesting world to another. I had left broadcasting for good, I thought, in March 1956. I remember vowing as I walked from the old familiar WGN studio in Chicago, "I'll never, as long as I live, sit in front of another microphone." (I had not, at that time, learned never to use the word "never.")

Earlier that same month, I had written and recorded a talk entitled *The Strangest Secret*. I had done it on the advice of an acquaintance, never dreaming for an instant that I was setting in motion forces that were to sweep me into a new career of the most amazing kind. With absolutely no fanfare or advertising, strictly by word of mouth, that record began a movement that was to become an avalanche. Hundreds of thousands of copies of *The Strangest Secret* have been bought by people all over the free world. All by itself it began a new industry, and it continues to sell with undiminished volume to this day. And now its many brothers and sisters produced since that time are at work in thousands of homes and in companies from the smallest to the very largest.

In the spring of 1959, another acquaintance suggested at lunch that I write and narrate a daily radio program for syndication. I told him of my vow regarding radio, studios, and microphones and promptly forgot the matter. But later, during the summer, on a Canadian fishing trip with my son David, the memory of that conversation came to mind. And in the quiet, peaceful evenings in that beautiful setting, I began writing the radio programs that we later called *Our Changing World*. When I returned to Chicago, I recorded the programs I'd written and we sent them to a representative sampling of radio stations. Another avalanche!

In five years, *Our Changing World* grew to be the largest syndicated radio program in the history of broadcasting. And it all started because of a chance remark and a Canadian fishing trip.

In this book, we have tried to select from the radio broadcast scripts that touch on a wide range of human interests. Their subjects range from attitude, conformity, and honesty to using time wisely and the law of increase. We have tried to make of it a book which could be picked up at any time and opened at random but which would, at the same time, be a carefully indexed volume for the writer, student, lecturer, or other person intent upon a definite subject.

—Earl Nightingale

THE LAW OF
INCREASING RETURNS

No one has ever become poor by giving.

—Anne Frank

Here are a few thoughts that you can make your own, thoughts that will guarantee you success all the years of your life. Now, that is quite a statement, but it's true.

To begin, let us understand that growth and increase are a part of mankind and all of nature. It is inherent in each of us to desire more. This is not wrong; it is perfectly natural and the way it should be. This is true of all of us—the members of our families, our friends, and associates, our customers. You should want to get rich in every department of your life.

But what do I mean by "rich"? Getting rich, for you, is getting what you want very much. For some, it means a bigger income or a large sum of capital. That is fine. You can get it without hurting, or even competing with, any other person. In fact, you can thereby increase the general well-being of everyone with whom you come in contact.

Unfortunately, the uninformed believe that you can get ahead in the world only at the expense of someone else. This is not true. No one can become rich in any way without enriching others. Anyone who adds to prosperity must prosper in turn.

Getting rich, for you, may mean obtaining more love, greater peace of mind, owning the home of your dreams, or accomplishing something else you've set your heart upon. In short, getting rich is getting whatever it is you want very much. It's as simple as that.

The first step is to understand completely that it is right for you to want what you want. All human activities are based on the desire for increase—people seeking more food, more clothes, more knowledge, more pleasure, more life.

The next step is to understand that you need not compete with or deprive anyone. Don't compete—create! In this way, you add to the general well-being without taking anything away from anyone.

Remember to give to every person more than you take from them. Now at first this may sound absurd, so let us dig into it a little. In order for a business or person to grow—and remember, growth is the natural desire of mankind—we must give more in use value than we charge. A building nail doesn't cost much, yet its use is great and goes on for years. This book didn't cost much; yet if you can get ideas from it that can bring you more than you now have, its use value will greatly exceed its cost.

How much does it cost to give love, respect, and consideration to those near you? Very little, just a little extra effort. Yet love, respect, and consideration are priceless to the person receiving them. This is the key: give more than you receive in everything you do. In this way, you are building a great credit for yourself which must come to you in some form, sooner or later. You are taking out less than you are putting in and by so doing are building a tidal wave of future prosperity.

This is the law of increasing returns. It is understood and followed undeviatingly by every successful businessperson, artist, professional, and worker and by every successful mother, father, and friend. It is the most striking attribute of all successful people, companies, and institutions.

Now, let us go back to creating instead of competing. You are the point from which all increase must stem, not your company, your marriage partner, your parents, or your friends. You are the creative center of your universe. Increase must come from you personally. Find ways of doing the things you do that reflect you and your own unique talents and abilities. If you do this, no other person in the world can operate exactly as you do. You will not be competing with anyone; you will be creating from within yourself.

As you find new and better ways of giving more in use value than you are receiving in money, more and more people will turn to you. You will find your circle of friends increasing. If you are in business, you will find it continually growing, expanding. Do this in a quiet and unobtrusive manner. You don't have to shout about how much you are doing for others. If you are doing more for others, they will recognize it and be drawn to you.

One of the most interesting things about such increase is that totally unexpected and wonderful things will begin to occur in your life.

People you don't know, who have exactly what you need, will make their appearance at the right time and the right place. Everything will begin to dovetail, and your life will take on new meaning and direction and bring you far greater rewards. Let the impression of growth, of increase, mark everything you do.

As you do these things, keep constantly before you the vision of what it is you intend to accomplish. Don't worry about it; just know you are going to accomplish it and, following these rules, you cannot fail.

OUR CHANGING WORLD

If a man empties his purse into his head,
no one can take it away from him.
An investment in knowledge always
pays the best interest.

—Benjamin Franklin

Machines become obsolete because they are unable to change. Times change—they must and will, with ever-accelerating momentum. As they do, the machines of today will be outdated. But human beings are not machines, however fond they are of acting like them; they can change.

Never before in the history of humankind has it been so necessary as it is today for us to develop a new awareness of ourselves with respect to our changing world. We need to face the fact that in the world of tomorrow, jobs will be radically different; many will be eliminated entirely. What can we do about it? We can take the advice of the former president of the University of Chicago, Robert M. Hutchins: "We can learn!" If we refuse to learn, and if we insist on acting like machines, we may find ourselves idle tomorrow.

Every job is part of a much larger organization. Organizations and industries don't die; they just change. The industry that once manufactured covered wagons is still here, but today it is making engines, tractors, and automobiles.

Let us say that through a set of circumstances, a young man finds himself working as an attendant in a service station. He might wish he had done things differently, but it does no good to brood over the past. These are the facts: he is working in a service station. He wants to get married and have a home and children. And to do this, he decides that he must earn more money. His first inclination is to look around for a job that pays more. But before he moves to a different job, he should be aware that the move entails not only earning more, but also learning a good deal more than he now knows. Otherwise, the chances are he will be no better off than he is pumping gas.

I think that instead of just looking at his job, he should look at the whole industry of which it is a part. In our example, this is the petroleum industry, one of the world's largest and most profitable. Without leaving his job for the present, he could spend his free time studying the industry he is already in. Now, instead of being a service station attendant, he is a trainee in a major industry. He no longer has just a job; he has his foot on the first rung of what can be a fine and extremely rewarding career. By sticking with his studies and doing an outstanding job when he is working, he will soon be able to marry and have that home and, in time, anything else he wants. Learning is the answer.

The same thing applies to the person working in the supermarket, the local factory, or as a salesperson. Naturally, it is best to stay in school, for school is the best place to learn. But for those who have dropped out, the answer is the same: Learn! Learn all you can and keep learning, whether you are 16 or 60, and you will find your way— a way infinitely more interesting and substantially more rewarding— in this changing world of ours.

The minute a person stops learning, our world will begin to pass them by. They will be left a lonely and disconsolate figure in its wake. To learn or not to learn is a decision each of us must make.

YOUR PRIVATE GOLD MINE

More gold has been mined from the brains
of men than has ever been taken from the earth.

—Napoleon Hill

From time to time, you hear somebody say, "You know, those people who got in on the ground floor of the opening of the West, with its gold and silver, really were fortunate. All that gold lying around, waiting to be baled and carried to market!" Or, you will hear: "And what about the early discoverers of our vast oil fields? All those derricks pumping millions of dollars' worth of black gold, and the folks who discovered it just sitting back and trying to keep their fortunes figured to the nearest millions!" When I was a youngster during the Depression, we used to sit around and dream of things like that. Maybe you've done the same thing.

Well, there is one place that is virtually unexplored, where you can find all the wealth you'll ever need. Perhaps you never thought much about it, but each of us has our own private gold mine, all staked out, with a clear title, just waiting to be developed.

Try to get a mental picture of a gold mine or an oil field before it is discovered. No busy, noisy machinery; no crowds of men; no trucks and heavy equipment—just land covered with prairie grass and stretching as far as the eye can see to the distant horizon. Now, under that peaceful and innocent-looking piece of prairie is a wide, deep lake of oil, or a mother lode of gold worth millions. But you'd never know it was there, would you? Before the treasured oil or gold was discovered, thousands of people must have rode and walked right over it without realizing that right under their feet was a king's ransom—riches beyond their wildest dreams.

Somebody had to come along looking for it. Someone had to be willing to risk digging for it. Somebody had to suspect it was there and start looking. Their chances of hitting pay dirt with their first shovelful were pretty slim, but they believed that if they kept looking, kept digging, they would find it.

You and I have free title to the richest continent on earth. It is called the human mind, and it has produced just about everything you see and hear around you. It comes as standard equipment at birth and maybe that is why most of us never use it: we don't value things we get free. Your mind has approximately 12 billion cells, and fully 90 percent of it has never been explored.

The greatest thing on earth is a good idea. Consider the man who got the idea to dig under that prairie grass. Discovering a fortune was only the effect. His idea to dig was the cause. It was his idea that resulted in millions of dollars for him.

Now, how many ideas do you think you could get in a single day—20 or 30? Let us say you got 20 ideas a day. That would be 100 a week if you didn't think on weekends. That would be 5,200 ideas a year—5,200 holes you would be drilling. Remember: one idea can make you rich!

If you know anything about the law of averages, you will realize that before long, you will have the idea you have been looking for. If the first 10 or first 100 are no good, don't give up. The more the dry holes, the closer you are to what you are looking for—your Big Idea, the one that will change your life!

Chances are that right now, as Russell Conwell used to say, you are standing in the middle of your acre of diamonds. What you are looking for is the idea that is bigger than you are—one that will keep you challenged and interested for a long time to come.

GREENER PASTURES

Small opportunities are often the beginnings of great enterprises.
—Demosthenes

The other day, I was reading about our universe and what we know and don't know about it—about the billions and billions of stars and planets and of the millions of galaxies like our Milky Way, separated by voids so vast it takes light (which travels 186,000 miles per second) about 2 million years to cross these almost incomprehensible distances. There are astronomers today sitting in front of telescopes looking at stars, not as they are now, but as they were 500 million years ago. That is how long it took the light from these stars to reach us, give or take a few years!

I have a hunch I know why astronomers and scientists are so curious, as we all are, about other worlds and other galaxies. It is partly because of what I call "greener pastures." The hope seems to spring eternal in all human beings that the opportunities are greater elsewhere. I suspect this uniquely human attribute, or frailty, has been at the root of all discovery.

But it is a saddening fact that many people spend so much time thinking of other pastures that they never properly appraise their own. While we are looking at what the other guy is doing and wishing we were in his pasture, others are wishing they were in ours. There is more opportunity hidden in our daily work than most of us could exploit in a lifetime. We need only look for it thoroughly enough, long enough to find it.

It is like the story of the African farmer who sold his farm and spent the rest of his life hunting for diamonds the world over, only to have the richest diamond mine in the world discovered on the farm he had sold.

There is no such thing as a job that cannot, with time and thought, lead to greatness. But unless we spend the time, study, and effort to become outstanding at what we are now doing, why in the world should we think we could become great at something else? Somehow, succeeding always looks easier in the other fellow's line of work. It once looked so good to me that I too climbed the fence out of my pasture. By the time I had scrambled back in again, my little excursion had cost me $30,000. I had gone into a business where I was short on experience and, as usually happens in such cases, I got burned on the wallet.

Now, I am not saying that you cannot go into a different business but rather that you should first learn everything possible about it. And more important still, look long and carefully at the pasture you are now in. Chances are it is loaded with opportunity that someone else is going to profit by if you don't.

If you merely compete with everyone else in your line, you must be satisfied with the same returns, the same rewards, they are getting. But if you create, the sky is the limit. With the opportunities and experience you already have, you can build a stairway to just about anything you want.

THE ROAD TO PEACE OF MIND

Men are often capable of greater things than they perform.
They are sent into the world with bills of credit,
and seldom draw to their full extent.

—Horace Walpole

Experts in human psychology say you cannot change your whole personality. It represents a complex of too many long-established, conditioned reflexes and behavior patterns—all those things that distinguish you as an individual. But regardless of the personality you have (and it's probably better than you think), you can be content with yourself and your world. The way to achieve this peace of mind is to develop yourself as fully as possible. Each of us has a ceiling of performance. This ceiling is high in the areas in which you excel and low in the areas in which you have little or no aptitude. And your peace of mind or dissatisfaction is directly related to how far you develop your own abilities and aptitudes. If you knew how to use yourself fully, you would know complete contentment. If you find yourself discontented, you should realize that it reflects your unfulfilled potential.

It might be a good idea to ask yourself just how much of your potential you think you are using. Would you say that you are operating at 50 percent of your total potential...30 percent...75 percent...10 percent? Estimate the figure. The individual who spends Saturday at home working on a new patio or in the garden is usually much happier, more cheerful, and more contented on Saturday night than the individual who spends the day on the sofa. The person whose job makes them work close to their potential is a much happier person, as a rule, than the person doing a job that does not exercise their creative and critical faculties. Contentment comes to us when we become conscious of our powers and our abilities.

It is important that each of us has a mental picture of the person we want to become and that we try day by day to come a little closer to fitting that picture. This gets rid of boredom and ennui, just as it gets rid of feelings of inferiority caused by working too far below our potential. And when you are dissatisfied, it is a good idea not to blame the work you do but rather the way you do it. Almost any job can offer a challenge if we attempt to do it superbly.

So if you find yourself discontented, examine the way in which you spend your days. The problem can usually be found there. Remember the great lines by Dean Briggs? "Do your work. Not just your work and no more, but a little more for the lavishing's sake—that little more which is worth all the rest. And if you doubt, as you must; and if you suffer, as you must—do your work. Put your heart into it and the sky will clear. And then out of your very doubt and suffering will be born the supreme joy of life."

Sometimes we seem to be concentrating so hard on reducing the workweek that we forget the joys and satisfactions of life found only in our work.

THE PHANTOM WALL

Courage consists, not in blindly overlooking danger,
but in seeing and conquering it.

—Jean Paul Richter

Have you ever stopped to think about how much people could have, know, and do if they would only try? When timidity, self-consciousness, and vague memories of past failures all contrive to erect a phantom wall between us and the things we would like to have or do, we need courage to leap or painfully clamber over it and achieve our desires.

Emerson wrote: "What a new face courage puts on everything! A determined man, by his very attitude and the tone of his voice, puts a stop to defeat and begins to conquer."

Courage is often a matter of simple logic. Say a boy at a high school prom refrains from asking a girl to dance. He's afraid she might say "no," but he hasn't thought his problem through. By not asking her, he achieves the same result he would if he asked and she said "no." The chances are excellent that she is dying to have someone ask. But the boy refuses to risk success. The same can be true of success in later life. Men and women rule out the possibility of winning by refusing to risk defeat. They don't seem to realize that a lack of courage guarantees failure.

I remember a story about a man running toward a broad river. As he reached a dock, he increased his speed; and when he came to the end of the dock, he threw himself as far out over the river as he could. He landed in the water about ten feet from the dock, swam back, and climbed out. An amazed bystander asked him why he jumped into the river. He answered that a friend of his had bet him $1,000 to one that he could not jump across the river, and after a while he just couldn't stand thinking about those odds without at least trying.

Many things that look impossible from a distance become quite feasible once we muster the courage to make an attempt. There is always a way to reach everything desirable. If the man who tried to jump across the broad river had traveled upstream to its source, he would have found that he could step across it and win his bet.

Emerson said: "He has not learned the lesson of life who does not every day surmount a fear." And he gave a good reason for this when he said: "Fear always springs from ignorance." And again: "Men suffer all their life long under the foolish superstition that they can be cheated. But it is as impossible for a man to be cheated by anyone but himself as for a thing to be and not to be at the same time."

Yes, we cheat ourselves of the lives we could know, the things we could accomplish, the things we could have, because we're afraid to try, to ask. If we but knew ourselves better and the nature of the world, we would fear less and attempt much more.

Why not realize your ambition? If you really want it, if it is right, if it will not hurt another, then abandon yourself to it with the attitude and conviction of courage and it will be yours.

ON BECOMING INDISPENSABLE

There's a man in the world who is never turned down,
wherever he chances to stray;
he gets the glad hand in the populous town,
or out where the farmers make hay;
he's greeted with pleasure on deserts of sand,
and deep in the aisles of the woods;
wherever he goes there's a welcoming hand—
he's the man who delivers the goods.

—Walt Whitman

Have you ever heard a man or woman say, "Well, it may not be much of a job, but at least it represents security"? This way of looking at things is probably a hangover from the Depression of the thirties. And it seems this word "security" has come to mean the wrong thing to most people. In the first place, there probably is not a job in the world that offers security. If you have a job, any one of a hundred things could happen to cause you to lose it. But there is a form of real security anybody can develop, and once you have it, it can never be lost again.

If a man loses the one thing he believes represents security, he has lost everything. He finds himself suddenly in a cold and hostile world. He feels lost and doesn't know which way to turn. If you are old enough to remember the Depression, you know what I mean. There were millions of people with vacant expressions on their faces, wondering what hit them, queuing up in long lines at employment offices, waiting for a job to open up—any job—and in the meantime, chinning themselves on the relief rolls. The jobs these people had certainly did not represent security; they had folded early in the general economic slump.

All of us want a degree of safety for ourselves and our families in this changing world. If a job won't provide it, what will? Security is being an expert at what you do for a living. Security is being an uncommon person. Security is the greatness anyone can have if they will develop it. Security is never outside a person. If it isn't within, it isn't anywhere.

When you're around someone who has security inside of them, you can feel it when they enter the room, and you can see it in the way they walk and hear it in the way they talk. They are an expert at their business, and they know it. While most people are doing just as little as they can to get by, the secure individual is working and studying and planning and growing with their industry and their country. They do not feed on the economy; they contribute to it.

No matter what a person's job happens to be at this moment, it is loaded with opportunity—if they'll just look for it! If they will think about their work and constantly come up with ways to improve it, become better at it, in an almost unbelievably short time they will become practically indispensable. Their company will start giving them more and more responsibility. When times are bad, they will always be the last one to be laid off. And if that should happen to them, they can always find a place for the unusual skills and ability they have developed.

This is security—this, and knowing enough to save at least 10 percent of your gross income, especially when times are good. Then, if something should happen to slow you down for a while, you are in a position to find the circumstances you want.

IT ISN'T THE JOB—IT'S YOU

Imagination is more important than knowledge.
—Albert Einstein

Have you ever wondered why one person will make an outstanding success at the same job or business that another person will fail in?

While I was having lunch with an old friend, we got on this subject, and it reminded him of a story about a distant relative. It seems this man found himself in Los Angeles right in the middle of the Depression of the thirties. For some reason, he decided to go into the real estate business. So, he took care of the necessary preliminaries and opened a small office in Los Angeles on a street known as "Real Estate Row."

For a month, this man sat in his office waiting for someone to come around to buy or sell some real estate. No one did. He began to notice that none of the other real estate offices were doing any business either; they were in fact dying on the vine. It was the time of a widespread depression and no one was buying much of anything.

Three months passed while he tried to think of ways to keep from starving to death. One day, he hit upon an idea. On the big "Real Estate" sign in front of his office, he wrote down at the bottom in small, conservative letters these words: "WE DO NOT HANDLE HOMES UNDER $25,000." Almost immediately, business began to come in. People who had homes valued at $25,000 and more began dropping in, asking him to sell their homes. He called only on people who could afford $25,000 homes (and there were still quite a few around, although they represented a microscopic minority in those days), and he began to sell. He had restricted his business to the only people in the area who could buy and sell homes. And they, quite naturally, only wanted to do business with the real estate operator who catered to the kind of deals they were interested in. To make a long story short, he was very successful and actually became quite wealthy—even during the Depression—in one of the hardest hit industries.

While real estate men all over town were crying on each other's shoulders about how terrible business was and how bad the times were, one man thought his way out of the dilemma. Anyone, in any job or business, can do this. The very fact that you have a problem means there must be a solution. This isn't Pollyannaish; this is good, sound, successful business, and it's being demonstrated every day.

Some time ago, I made a speech at the University of Georgia. The gentleman sitting next to me at the speakers' table told me we were in the heart of what has become the chicken-producing center of the country. He went on to say that some years back, the area was deeply depressed until one man got the idea of giving eggs to farmers to incubate and raise chickens. All they had to buy was the feed, and he would sell their chickens for them. He made money, the farmers made money, and the entire area boomed. If there's a problem, there's a solution, if you can just think of the idea for it. And as "Red" Motley says, "There's nothing in the world more powerful than an idea whose time has come."

No matter what we achieve, it consists of solving problems. But I think that too often we underestimate our own powers. You can solve problems just as well as the next person. Half the battle is knowing they can be solved.

HOW'S THE WORLD TREATING YOU?

Tis a very good world we live in,
To spend, and to lend, and to give in;
But to beg, or to borrow, or ask for our own,
Tis the very worst world that ever was known.

—J. Bromfield

We live in a world of words. We have a word for everything, and some of these names and labels mean a great deal to us. Words such as "love," "happiness," "success," "achievement," "joy," and "ability" describe conditions all of us want, but there is one word that controls them all. That is, there is one word that describes a condition that will bring us all of these things or keep us from getting any one of them.

If your youngster asked what this word is, could you tell him? If, from all of the many thousands of words in the language, you were asked to select the one that would influence your life more than any other, could you pick the right word? I call it the "magic word," and it is

"ATTITUDE!" Once we are grown and on our own, this word actually controls our environment, our entire world.

If you are curious about what kind of an attitude you have, a simple test will tell you what it has been up to this point in your life. Just answer this question with a "yes" or "no": "Do you feel the world is treating you well?" If your attitude toward the world is good, you will obtain good results. If your attitude is excellent, excellent will be your results. If your attitude is negative, little that is positive awaits you. And if your attitude is just so-so, you will live in a world that is not particularly bad, nor particularly good, just so-so.

Our environment, which is another way of saying how the world treats us, is nothing more than a reflection—a mirror, actually—of our own attitude.

One of the most pitiful aspects of society is the really large percentage of people who lead dismal, narrow, darkened lives, crying out against what appears to be a cruel world, which they believe has singled them out for a lifetime of trouble, misery, and bad luck. Those who find themselves in such a prison of discontent should face the fact that they have very probably built their prison with their own hands. And unless they change, their cell will continue to grow smaller and darker.

The world doesn't care whether we change or not. Adopting a good, healthy attitude toward life doesn't affect life and the people with whom we come in contact nearly as much as it affects us. As it says in the Bible: "As ye sow, so shall ye reap."

It would be impossible even to estimate the number of jobs that have been lost, the number of promotions missed, the number of sales not made, the number of marriages ruined by poor attitudes. But you can number in the millions the jobs that are held but hated, the marriages that are tolerated but unhappy, all because of people who are waiting for others, or the world, to change toward them, instead of being big enough and wise enough to realize that we only get back what we put out.

In 30 days, you can change your world and your environment by taking this simple test. For 30 days, treat every person you meet, without a single exception, as the most important person on earth. You will find that they will begin treating you the same way. You see, every person, as far as he or she is concerned, is the most important person on earth. How does the world look at you? Exactly as you look at the world.

WHEN YOUR DREAMS DIE

*As I approve of a youth that has something of the old man
in him, so I am no less pleased with an old man that has
something of the youth. He that follows this rule may
be old in body, but can never be so in mind.*

—Cicero

How would you like a recipe for staying young? From the earliest times, humans have believed that their search for a fountain of youth would be rewarded. They have sought it much as an individual goes in search of happiness. And they have found that the secrets of both youth and happiness lie in the same place: within themselves.

A philosopher once wrote, "There is not much to do but bury a man when the last of his dreams is dead." That seems to be the answer—a person is as young as his dreams—for it explains why some people are old at 40, others still young at 90.

Youth is a time for tackling new projects, and as long as a person is enthusiastically beginning something new, they will remain young in the only places that really count—in their mind and heart. They will be young in spirit. As Emerson said, "We need not count a man's years until he has nothing else to count."

The person who has no dream to spur them on, no goal to achieve, is already old, for age comes when hope and planning for the future die. This is why an individual's lifework must be much larger than an eight-hour-a-day job. People grow old only in occupations with fixed limitations, uninteresting surroundings, and with no call upon the imagination or the mind.

But some individuals stay young, regardless of their work. These are the people who are striving for something better, something greater. People who stay young are people who feel young, regardless of their years. They are people who like to try new things and like working toward a goal, whether they live long enough to reach it or not.

People who stay young never think much about old age or death. They concern themselves less with what might lie beyond the pale and more with the here and now, with today and tomorrow and next week. You'll never find them poring over the obituaries to see whom they have outlasted.

People who stay young keep their sense of humor; they know how to laugh, even when the joke happens to be on them. They do not hold grudges; if they are angered by something or someone, they are quick to forgive and forget. They seem to know that hatred hurts only the hater.

People who stay young look for and are quick to accept new ideas. They have a healthy curiosity about everything that comes within the range of their senses. They know that while they may slow down considerably from a physical standpoint, the mind can grow more able, more powerful with the years. A person can be at their best mentally at 80, or even older.

But above all, they continue in pursuit of a dream—something to earn or bring about; a new, higher plateau upon which to stand. Titian was painting masterpieces when he was 98. What is the dream you are trying to bring to fulfillment? A person is as young as their dreams and as old as their doubts.

THE FLYWHEEL OF SOCIETY

*If you want something new, you have
to stop doing something old.*

—Peter F. Drucker

William James, in his *Principles of Psychology*, defined "genius" as "little more than the faculty of perceiving in an unhabitual way." In his essay on habit, he referred to habit as the "flywheel of society"—the thing that keeps us doing what we have been doing in the past, the thing that makes us fear change regardless of the present condition of our lives. And the genius, as defined by Dr. James, seems to be that rare bird who knows that change is not only good, but inevitable. He anticipates the inevitable. It is he perhaps who makes change inevitable. He takes nothing for granted. He knows that whatever he sees that is made by man or served by man is imperfect, is always in the state of evolving.

Let me give you an example. A friend of mine was seeking a site for a large luxury motel. He was in no hurry and spent months in a large West Coast city looking for the site that would probably best guarantee a good return on the considerable amount of money he was going to invest and borrow. He found the perfect site. It was near a large university and at the intersection of five main roads, two of which were very heavily traveled. It was also within the city limits, which would mean a large local trade for the restaurant. There was only one hitch: on the site stood an old brick building housing a manufacturing concern that was still in business.

He called on the owners of the business and told them what he wanted to do. Since the city had, over the years, grown around the old building, he pointed out that it would be to their benefit to sell him the property at a price many times the land's original value and build themselves a new, modern plant in a less congested area. They saw the sense of his plan and a way to get nearly half a million dollars for their property. The deal was closed. He razed the building and built his motel.

Later, he discovered that many people in the motel business had looked upon that site as ideal for their purposes but had written it off because it was already occupied. The point is that he saw it, not with the old brick manufactory on it, but instead with his beautiful new motel sitting there; he looked at that corner in an unhabitual way. And everybody benefited by his genius, including the community.

I think each of us can greatly increase the value of our life by taking to heart Dr. James's definition of genius; by looking at the things about us—in our home and particularly in our work—with new eyes, with the eyes of creation. We can form the habit of seeing things, not as they are, but as they perhaps will be, as they could be, as our changing world insists they be. Our lives are full of old brick buildings that we assume will remain standing where they are. And maybe they always will, if we don't do something about them.

HOW TO GET WHAT YOU WANT

Thought in the mind hath made us.
What we are by thought was wrought and built.

—James Allen

I receive many letters from men and women all over the country who say they want to be successful but don't know how. They have tried following all sorts of involved rules, yet they really need only one. Sir Isaac Newton was once asked how he discovered the law of gravitation; he replied, "By thinking about it all the time." There is your answer—the only one you need: "By thinking about it all the time."

Each of us becomes what we think about. So, if you can say what it is you spend most of your time thinking about, you can tell yourself what it is you are going to become. If that is not what you really want, you can change your destiny.

Consciously—or, as is more commonly the case, unconsciously—each of us forges our own life and becomes great, good, average, fair, or poor. The late Mike Todd, the motion picture producer who made and lost millions and then made them back again, was once asked if it didn't worry him to invest so much of his own money in a deal where he could lose it all. He answered to the effect that being broke is a temporary situation but poverty is a state of mind.

But just thinking and never doing will not help you get what you're looking for. Thought without action is as useless as action without thought. The person who makes up their mind to reach a high and difficult goal must, in order to achieve it, do a great many things. But it is their constant thought that leads them to make it a reality.

By looking at what any individual past 40 or 50 has accomplished, you can tell what they have spent most of their time thinking about. Marshall Field, one of the world's most successful businessmen, had 12 rules for success, but none of them is worth much if a person does not know, and does not constantly think about, the goal they have decided to reach. Here are the 12 things Mr. Field would urge you to remember:

1. The value of time
2. The success of perseverance
3. The pleasure of working
4. The dignity of simplicity
5. The worth of character
6. The power of kindness
7. The influence of example
8. The obligation of duty
9. The wisdom of economy
10. The virtue of patience
11. The improvement of talent
12. The joy of originating

Your life is controlled by your thoughts. Your thoughts are controlled by your goals. Have you set your goals yet?

MAKE NEW FRIENDS AS YOU GO

Today is not yesterday. We ourselves change. How then,
can our works and thoughts, if they are always to be the fittest,
continue always the same? Change, indeed, is painful, yet ever needful;
and if memory have its force and worth, so also has hope.

—Thomas Carlyle

In replying to the tributes paid to him at a testimonial dinner, Herbert Bayard Swope once said, "I cannot give you the formula for success, but I can give you the formula for failure: try to please everybody."

One mistake made by most people is to believe you should keep all your friends all your life. It cannot be done. It should not be done! H. L. Mencken said, "A prudent man, remembering that life is short, examines his friendships critically now and then. A few he retains, but the majority he tries to forget."

On the same subject, Bernard Shaw wrote, "The only man who behaves sensibly is my tailor; he takes my measure anew each time

49

he sees me, while all the rest go on with their old measurements and expect them to fit me." Living means changing, and changing means, or at least should mean, forming new friendships and discarding some of those we outwear. No two people mature at the same rate; some move ahead faster than others, and it is just ridiculous to try to retain all of our old friendships. Yet people often feel guilty about outgrowing a friendship; they think they are becoming snobbish or being disloyal when actually it is perfectly natural.

I do think that when we get older, we form stronger and more lasting friendships than when we were young, changing, and moving around a lot. Our best and most lasting friendships are those with people who think along the same lines, believe in the same things, and constantly challenge us to move ahead with them into increasing mental and emotional maturity. They are friends with whom we enjoy spending an evening, with a lot of good conversation over dinner and, maybe, far into the night. Every time I spend a weekend with a certain friend of mine in St. Louis, or when he comes to visit me, we sit up until dawn discussing one thing or another. We disagree violently on several issues, and it makes for really lively conversations. We may outgrow this friendship someday, but I know we will not until it is best for both of us to move ahead to other new and equally interesting associations. Having good old friends is wonderful, but in some ways it is even better to look forward to the new ones.

KEEP MOVING

By the streets of "by and by" one arrives at the house of "never."
—Miguel de Cervantes

Have you ever noticed that the longer you put off something you should do, the more difficult it is to get started?

Ironically, we deliberately add to the frustration and unhappiness we could so clearly avoid. The great newspaper editor Arthur Brisbane once wrote: "Don't exaggerate your own importance, your own size, or your own miseries. You are an ant in a human anthill. Be a working ant, not a ridiculous insect pitying yourself."

Strong language, maybe, but it has a lot of sense for us. A person carrying a heavy weight is all right as long as he keeps going. The minute he stops, puts the weight on the ground, and sits down to rest, the weight seems to become heavier, the distance to be traveled greater, and the work just that much more unpleasant.

It can seem at times that things have piled up so high there's just no way of digging out—but there is. Pick the task that is most crucial and simply begin! Just by plunging in you will feel better, and you will find that the water is not nearly as cold as you thought it would be. Keep at it, and before long the pile of things that seemed so overwhelming is behind you—finished.

It isn't the work itself that overwhelms us; it's thinking about how hard it is going to be. It's seeing it get larger every day. It's putting it off and hoping that somehow, through some miracle, it will disappear. There is a saying that a journey of a thousand miles begins with but a single step. And that step accomplishes two things. First, it shortens the distance we still have to travel. Second, and just as important, it instills hope; it strengthens our faith. If a person will just keep putting one foot in front of the other, they will be taken into new and exciting places and think thoughts that never would have come to them if they'd remained at the starting point. Then, when the journey is finished, they wonder how or why they could ever have sat so long and worried so much.

If you'll think back, you'll remember the contentment you have experienced after finishing a difficult piece of work or facing up to a responsibility you were worried about. It's never as bad as you think it's going to be, and the joy that will come with its accomplishment makes it more than worthwhile. Work never killed anyone. It's worry that does the damage, and the worry would disappear if we would just settle down and do the work. An American president said: "All growth depends upon activity. There is no development physically or intellectually without effort, and effort means work."

And it never hurts to do a little something extra just for the lavishing's sake. Elbert Hubbard put it this way: "People who never do any more than they're paid to do are never paid for any more than they do." Payment comes in many forms—but always in exact proportion to what we do.

THAT'S WHAT THEY'RE TRYING TO DO

The best way to make children good
is to make them happy.

—Oscar Wilde

I remember hearing an angry father shout at his 12-year-old son, "Why don't you grow up?" There was a sudden silence in the room, and then the boy, his face working to control his tears, quietly said, "That's what I'm trying to do."

That's presumably what all young people are trying to do, and it's not an easy job. As adults, we tend be impatient with others who cannot do as well, as quickly, something that took us perhaps years to learn— if, indeed, we have completely learned it ourselves.

To the skillful, the fumbling, awkward attempts of the novice often seem ludicrous or exasperating, if not totally incomprehensible. "No, no," we say, "that's not the way to do it!" And in we charge to take over. In doing so, we add humiliation and self-consciousness to the beginner's feelings of inadequacy. When we humiliate people by

SUCCESSFUL LIVING *in a* **CHANGING WORLD**

treating them as though they were inept, bungling fools, they will begin to hate us. And each time we jump on them again—each time we tell them how inadequate they are with such remarks as "Won't you ever learn?" or "You're impossible!" or "You can't do anything right!" or "Why don't you grow up?"—we feed a little additional fuel to the fire.

If someone talked to us that way, we'd punch him in the nose, but youngsters can't do that, much as they'd love to. The fire just builds within them. They're terribly disappointed in the parent and in themselves. They're torn by the wish to love, the need to love, and the hate they feel. This is the kind of tumultuous inner battle that an adult finds most difficult to handle and resolve. In a child, or a very young person, when everything in life looms so much bigger, so much more final and terrible, it takes on catastrophic proportions.

Later, when the young person has grown into adulthood and, hopefully, some degree of maturity, he and his parent, or parents, may become friends again. He may even make exactly the same mistakes with his kids. It's a costly shame that we use a double standard in dealing with our children and with other people. Not all parents do; some parents treat their youngsters with courtesy, respect, and love and, at the same time, lay down firm guidelines and rules of conduct.

Being a good parent must surely be one of the world's most difficult jobs, exceeded in difficulty only by the process of growing up itself. It's a job for which most of us had no training and little more than the resolution to try to do a better job than our parents did with us. But if there's a key word to successful child-rearing, I rather imagine it's the same that is the cornerstone of successful marriage: *courtesy*. It's showing those we love and for whom we are responsible the common courtesy and respect we show to total strangers.

Living in close and constant proximity makes this difficult, perhaps, but no less necessary. When it comes to raising children, everyone thinks they're an expert, and I guess I'm no exception. But if we tried to follow the advice of all the so-called experts in this field, nothing we did would be right—except, maybe, using a little courtesy.

WHO'S YOUR BOSS?

Right or wrong, the customer is always right.
—Marshall Field

'll bet you could ask 1,000 working people the question "Who's your boss?" and never get the right answer. There is only one boss, and whether a person shines shoes for a living or heads the largest corporation in the world, his boss remains the same. It is the customer. Here is the one person who pays everyone's salary and who decides whether a business is going to succeed or fail. He doesn't care if a business has been around 100 years; the minute it starts treating him badly, he'll put it out of business.

This boss, the customer, is actually the one who buys everything you have or will ever own. He has bought all of your clothes, your car, your home, pays for your children's education and your vacations. He pays all of your bills, and he pays them in exact proportion to the way you treat him. The man who works deep inside a big plant on an assembly line might think he is working for the company that writes his paycheck, but he is not. He is working for the person who buys the product that comes off the end of the line. If the person doesn't like the product, he will not buy it, and eventually, if this continues, in effect he fires the man on the assembly line. In fact, he will fire everyone in the company from the president on down. He can do it by simply spending his money on some other product.

This is one of the reasons why taking pride in the work we do is so important to us personally. Aside from the joy that comes from doing an exceptionally good job, it will help get more customers, keep the ones we have, and ensure the weekly paycheck. I once patronized a launderer that kept breaking buttons on my shirts. I no longer send the shirts to them. There must be hundreds of men who have had the same experience with this particular launderer. Eventually—and it may have already happened—the person running the press, who kept breaking the buttons, has to lose that job. The customer loses, the company loses, the employee loses. This doesn't help anyone.

Some companies that had large, flourishing businesses a few years ago are no longer in existence. They couldn't, or didn't, satisfy the customer; they forgot who the boss really is. Some brand names that once were famous, that were leaders in their fields not so long ago, have disappeared; others are bigger and better than ever. The customer is always fair. He can be won back, if you don't let him go too long. He will spend his money with you if you earn it, and he will bring his friends.

You can get in your car and drive across the country and tell by looking at any business, from a little corner grocery store to a mammoth corporation, exactly how it is treating the boss by seeing the way the boss has been treating the business.

Knowing who the boss really is and how to treat him can make all the difference—not only between success and failure but also between happiness and frustration.

THE ART OF LISTENING

*The great charm of conversation consists less
in the display of one's own wit and intelligence than in
the power to draw forth the resources of others.*

—Jean de La Bruyère

Bennett Cerf tells of a college professor, much admired in his field, who would often invite his more promising students to his home for informed get-togethers. On one such occasion, an eager sophomore asked: "Professor, what's the secret of the art of good conversation?" The professor held up an admonishing finger and said, "Listen." After a long minute had passed, the sophomore said, "Well, I'm listening." And the professor said, "That is the secret."

It is also something that we would do well to check ourselves on from time to time. What brought this to mind was a luncheon I recently suffered through in the company of a person who obviously had never taken the time to learn the secret of the art of conversation. I am sure you know the type. He can be recognized by his rapidly moving mouth from which issues little or nothing of value. He seems to feel there is something wrong with silence and reflection.

Someone else has said that good conversation is like a tennis match in which the subject of conversation is lobbed back and forth, with everyone participating. But with those who have not learned this valuable art, you are more like a spectator at a golf match, simply standing by while some fellow keeps hitting his own ball.

These are times when you would like to have a tape recorder and a hidden microphone so you could send the conversation-dominator a recording of his one-way diatribe. Then he could hear himself riding roughshod over others, curtly dismissing their comments and churning back into his own stream of sound like a hippopotamus in a millpond.

Listening really is the key to good conversation. You can't learn much with your own mouth open. Whatever you say has to be something you already know...unless you are guessing or, worse still, faking, in which case you are riding for an embarrassing fall.

The most embarrassing moments I can recall have been the times I was talking when I should have been listening. So every once in a while, I remind myself to be a good listener. Then, when it is my turn to add something to the general conversation, perhaps I can add something of value or interest.

It's not an easy thing to do, especially when the conversation turns to a subject on which you have a strong opinion. There is a great temptation to jump in with both feet, flailing arms and working jaw, submerging the entire room in one's own great wisdom. But if one will summon the self-control and resist the urge, one can then parcel out their familiarity with the subject in small amounts. This permits others to share the topic. A person just might, through this method, manage to sound relatively intelligent all evening.

And if you run across a conversation hog, don't try to compete. If he runs down, which isn't likely, toss him another subject. You will find he is an expert on everything under the sun, and while he is talking, you can be thinking constructively of something else.

A WORD TO LIVE BY

Integrity is the first step to true greatness.

—C. Simmons

When General Dean was a prisoner of the communist Chinese in Korea and had been led to believe that he would soon be shot, he wrote a letter to his wife with instructions for their son. He wrote: "Tell Bill the word is *integrity*."

Here is the best advice a parent can give to a child. With that single word and realizing all that it means, a young man or woman can look forward to a tremendously rewarding life. It will mean living by the Golden Rule, an insurance policy that guarantees abundance.

Integrity is the quality we most often look for in others. It is what a woman wants in her husband, and he in her. It is what the boss wants of his or her employees, and vice versa. If you are having a home built, it is what you want most from the people who work on it, whether you are there to watch them or not. Integrity is the world's most valuable quality in a service, a product, or a person.

If people use the word *integrity* as a guide for all their dealings with others, they can rest easy in the knowledge that they will find it coming back to them in countless ways. One of the greatest rewards is the feeling of personal worth and the confidence and assurance that integrity brings.

The man or woman of integrity doesn't have to contend with a haunted house full of fears and worries. Since this person treats everyone with whom he comes in contact and everything he does with integrity, it will be reflected throughout his world.

There are probably millions of people who would not steal someone else's property but who think it is all right to give less than their best to their work. They don't think of this as stealing, but it is. What would you consider it if such a person were working to build your home? Frequently, our attitude changes with the situation. An incompetent waitress, out to dinner with her boyfriend, will be the first to complain about poor service. A sloppy builder will suspect a sloppy attitude toward something being built for him, and he will yell his head off if he finds it. We look for our own shortcomings in others. But the man or woman of integrity expects integrity in others as a matter of course. Over the long haul, the person who lacks integrity in any aspect of their life—at work, at home, or with their social contacts—is a person who has failed to mature. They lack wisdom, and they will suffer for it.

General Dean, undoubtedly, gave a lot of thought to the advice he wanted to leave his son. If he had thought for ten years, he could not have come up with a better word than *integrity*.

THE MOST
IMPORTANT THING

The spirit of truth and the spirit of freedom—
they are the pillars of society.

—Henrik Ibsen

Ask yourself: "What's the most important thing on earth as far as a human being is concerned?" I think it is truth. Truth is knowledge, and truth is honesty. To the extent that a person has knowledge and honesty, they are rich. Mirabeau once said: "If honesty did not exist, we ought to invent it as the best means of getting rich." Shakespeare wrote: "To be honest as the world goes, is to be one man picked out of ten thousand." Both of them were right.

To be ignorant is to be poor. It does not have to do with money, necessarily, although one seldom finds a person with knowledge who is not getting along well in the world. They may not be wealthy in the conventional sense, but they have enough for their needs, and they're enormously wealthy in many important ways. A person will enjoy life, the world, and people to the extent that they move away from ignorance and toward knowledge. Perhaps just as important, or even more so, the degree to which a person has truth and knowledge will determine their degree of freedom as an individual. Every human being has to be born ignorant and, for a time, live in ignorance. But if they remain ignorant, that is their own fault. The fight against ignorance waged by everyone during his or her lifetime must be an individual, personal thing. No one can give us truth. Another person can point out the truth and urge us to strive to make it our own, but it is far too great a thing to be received passively. It must be searched for actively if it is to have significance. We can be inspired to search for truth, but unless we find it for ourselves it will do us little good.

A strong man cannot make a weak man strong. But a weak man can make himself strong by following a planned course of action for a given time, and of course, a strong man can make himself stronger.

To my way of thinking, each of us has the opportunity for freedom and the wealth that comes with knowledge and understanding. If we decide to stop before we have reached our riches, we should blame no one but ourselves. I believe a man is poor to the extent that he is ignorant, because the riches and the freedom he seeks—if he is truly seeking them—are all around him. They are under his feet and perched on his shoulder; they are in public library and the corner bookstore. Truth and the riches it brings surround us every day of our lives. If we do not see them, we are poor indeed. Horace Mann put it this way: "Keep one thing forever in view—the truth; and if you do this, though it may seem to lead you away from the opinions of men, it will assuredly conduct you to the throne of God."

THE BELIEF BUTTON

*In actual life every great enterprise begins with
and takes its first forward step in faith.*

—Friedrich Schlegel

The other night over dinner I was talking to a good friend of mine, who is a hypnotist, about hypnosis and some of the amazing things that can be done with it. My friend pointed out that what hypnosis does is simply obtain a clear shot at a person's belief button. That is, a person hypnotized by someone who knows their business gets rid of all doubts and believes almost everything they are told.

Once a person believes they can do something, they can actually do it. That is why painless operations are possible under hypnosis—why even bleeding can be controlled. A hypnotized person can do amazing things that they would never do in a waking state. But a person can do nothing under hypnosis that they could not do in their waking state, if they only believed they could. We are not given new strength when we are hypnotized; strengths we already have are simply brought out. We are, however, so full of doubts—so suspicious of our own abilities—under normal circumstances that we operate far below our capabilities.

Here is but one example. A salesman had been employed by a major concern for seven years. During those seven years, his commissions had averaged $7,700 a year, a reasonable income—the kind of income a fairly hardworking salesman could expect to make. One day this salesman got the idea that he was not operating as efficiently as he could. He was sort of coasting along, doing a pretty average job, because that was what the other fellows were doing. He was earning more than some and less than others; he was accepted, and he was getting along.

He was not hypnotized, but because he received some inspiration to do better, he began really utilizing his time and ability. The first year following this decision, he almost tripled his income to more than $22,000. He added a swimming pool to his home, bought a new car, and took a trip to Europe all in that same year. This is a true story, and I have a letter to prove it. He had previously "hypnotized" himself into believing he was an average person (actually, there is no such thing) and had performed in accordance with what he believed himself to be.

As soon as his belief changed, as soon as he envisaged himself doing three times as well, he began to act this new part, and everything fell into place. Today, he is living a far more successful, interesting, and exciting life. He and his wife are enjoying all the things they used to dream about. This is not self-hypnosis; it is merely understanding that the picture we habitually hold of ourselves is far smaller than it could be. We know we can do amazing things under hypnosis simply because we believe we can. Why not maintain this belief in our waking state? This is what Socrates was talking about when he said, "Know thyself."

Most of us normally perform far below our capabilities simply because we lack faith in ourselves. This can be changed. The great line appears in Mark 9:23: "If thou canst believe, all things are possible to him that believeth."

HOW MUCH CAN YOU DO

We can do anything we want to do
if we stick to it long enough.

—Helen Keller

We all have read news stories from time to time telling of almost superhuman feats performed by people under the pressure of strong emotional stimuli. A 12-year-old boy lifted, off the legs of his father, a log so heavy that four men could hardly budge it later. A slender housewife, whose husband had been pinned beneath the car he was working on when it slipped off the jack, succeeded in raising one end of the car sufficiently for him to wriggle out. Seeing a truck driver trapped in the crushed and burning cab of his wrecked truck, a man crawled in through the window and, bracing his feet, put his back against the smashed top and raised it enough for rescuers to remove the driver. During a bombing attack in World War II, I saw a sailor jump from a platform high on the mast of a battleship and land on a steel turret far below without even spraining his ankle. Under normal conditions, he would have been killed or at least have broken the bones in his legs and hips.

The point I want to make is that we don't even know what our potential is until we are moved by some strong stimulus. I think this is why people who are in work they hate often do such a poor job and why people who are in work they love do so well. People with a burning desire to accomplish some ambitious goal do accomplish it, while others without a powerful emotional impetus behind their actions will fail at the same thing.

The people who go on to great success in the world do not accomplish their goals because they know somebody, or cheated somebody, or stepped on a competitor, or "got a break." I don't care what the cynics say; I have studied too many of these cases to be fooled. These people got to the top because they have to—because inside them burns a dream too big, too ever-present, too demanding to be denied. That is why it is foolish to suggest that they settle for less or that they are wrong in their drive for greatness. It is not that they just want to get to the top; they have to, and there's nothing in the world they can do about it. They would be miserable in any other kind of existence. They accomplish the seemingly impossible because of a great need—an emotional stimulus that forces them over every obstacle—that makes them begin again no matter how many failures they encounter along the way. They succeed simply because they insist on it.

SAVING: YOU'LL BE GLAD AND SORRY

The way to wealth depends chiefly
on industry and frugality.

—Benjamin Franklin

There is an old fable about a man who was riding across the desert at night. As he was crossing a dry riverbed, a voice came out of the darkness ordering him to halt. The voice then said, "Now get off your camel." The man got off, and the voice said, "Pick up some gravel from the riverbed." The man did. Then the voice said, "Now mount and ride on. In the morning, you'll be both glad and sorry." When it became light enough, the rider looked at what he had picked up from the riverbed and discovered it was not gravel at all—it was a handful of precious gems! And as the voice had said, he was both glad and sorry—glad he had picked up a few and sorry he had not picked up more. Like most fables, this one is based on human nature, and I guess it is particularly true right here in America.

I think we all realize that we are living in the richest country the world has ever known. As a matter of fact, we are right in the middle of the Golden Age of which man has dreamed since the days of

Pythagoras, Plato, and Aristotle. The American worker, compared with those in most other countries, is a wealthy man. Compare his income and standard of living to Americans of 50 years ago, and he is a regular tycoon!

But most modern American families are like the man in the fable who picked up the few precious stones, thinking they were gravel. They are glad they have such a high standard of living, but about 95 percent of them wind up sorry—sorry because they never woke up to the fact that financial independence has nothing at all to do with the money you are paid but only with the money you save!

Imagine 100 young Americans who all start even at age 25. Forty years later, when they are 65, only one out of the original 100 is well-to-do, four are financially independent for life, and the rest, the 95 percent, didn't make it. It is a little-known fact that regardless of what an individual happens to do for a living, they can be financially independent for life by the time they are 65 if they will only give a dime out of every dollar to the forgotten person—themselves—and the forgotten family—their own. The average American income is something around $7,000 a year. The average American works for 40 years. If they saved only ten cents out of every dollar they earned, they would save $24,000—not counting interest, which would more than double it.

Here is an interesting little test you can make. Take the number of years you have been married, times your income, times 10 percent. That is how much you should have in a permanent, never-touched savings program for your later years. If you have this amount or more in your savings account, you belong to the top 5 percent of the people in this country. If it is less, you are in the 95 percent boat. The latter is obviously a leaky boat. So by starting a systematic plan now and adding maybe 5 percent more of your income, you might be able to catch up pretty fast. As old Ben Franklin said, "The way to wealth is as plain as the way to market. Waste neither time, nor money, but make the best use of both." Unless you are saving at least 10 percent of your gross income, you may be making a serious mistake. Bernard Shaw once said: "I have no use for people who blame circumstances for their position in life. I like people who look for the circumstances they seek, and if they can't find them, make them!"

THE FARMER
AND THE PREACHER

There is a perennial nobleness, even sacredness in work.
Were he ever so benighted and forgetful of his high calling,
there is always hope in a man who actually and earnestly works.

—Thomas Carlyle

A favorite story of mine is the one about a preacher who was driving down a country road when he came upon the most magnificent farm he had ever seen in a life spent in rural preaching. The farm stood out like a diamond; it sparkled. Although it was by no means a new farm, the house and outbuildings were finely constructed and freshly painted. The garden around the house displayed a collection of beautiful flowers. A fine row of trees lined each side of the white-graveled drive. The fields were beautifully tilled, and a fine herd of fat dairy cattle grazed knee-deep in the pasture. All this comprised a beautiful painting of what the ideal farm should look like, and the preacher stopped to drink in the sight.

It was then he noticed the farmer on a big, shiny tractor, hard at work. As the farmer approached the spot where the preacher stood beside his car, the preacher hailed him. The farmer stopped his tractor, idled down the engine, and shouted a friendly, "Hello!" And the preacher said to him, "My good man, God has certainly blessed you with a magnificent farm." There was a pause as the farmer took off his billed cap and wiped the perspiration from his face with a bandana. He studied the preacher for a moment and then shifted in his seat to take a look around at his pride and joy. Then he turned back to the preacher and said, "Yes, he has, and we're grateful. But you should have seen this place when he had it all to himself!"

The preacher looked at the strong, friendly features of the farmer for a moment, smiled, and with a wave of his hand climbed back into his car and continued on his way. He heard the roar of the tractor's engine as the farmer returned to his work, and he thought, "That man has given me my sermon for next Sunday." He thought about the fact that every farmer along this road had been blessed with the same land, the same opportunity, and each worked his farm according to his nature. He understood that every farm, every home of every family in the country, was the living reflection of the people who lived there. He understood that the land we are given is not the acres we buy for a farm, or the lot on which we build a home, or the apartment we rent, but rather the life we've been blessed with. That's our plot of ground; that's the land we sow and from which we are then obliged to reap the resulting harvest.

The farmer he had seen would find abundant reward, not just when the time came to gather in his crops, but every time he looked around his place—every time he returned from town to that white-graveled drive, and the trees that lined it, and the fine home and gardens that waited at the end of it. He was grateful for what he had, but he knew that it is not what is given us that makes the difference but rather what we do with it—what we make of what we have.

A DEEPER PURPOSE

He that does good to another does good also to himself,
not only in the consequences but in the very act.
For the consciousness of well-doing is in itself ample reward.

—Lucius Annaeus Seneca

I have long held the belief that every business, no matter what its form or function, should have a purpose beyond that of profit and survival.

Naturally, the first responsibility of management, whether of a small neighborhood restaurant, a corner gas station, or a corporate giant, is to survive and grow. It must earn a profit, not only to satisfy its owner or its stockholders and directors but also to pump needed money into research, development, and expansion. It must earn a profit so that it can continue to pay the salaries of its employees and offer jobs to more people as the company grows. But it should also have an additional goal, a deeper purpose constantly before it, and this should be to upgrade all who are influenced by it. I am sure there are many who will smile at this sentiment, but there are also many who will not.

The fact is that those who take this idea most seriously are the managers of the world's most successful firms in every field of business. But in many businesses, this second purpose is ignored even if it is recognized or understood. This is precisely why the majority of businesses of all kind have to be classified as second rate; they lack the deeper purpose that must accompany greatness in anything. In fact, the not-uncommon slump or leveling off that comes to so many businesses after a long period of growth is often brought about by the abandonment of this deeper purpose.

For example, a business that begins with a purpose of providing the best product it can offer in its field may, 10 or 15 years later, be more concerned with saving costs and increasing profit margins. Many once-successful business firms have gone under because they became so involved in markets, competition, and pricing that they lost sight of the company's purpose, its reason for being. There is a saying that people remember quality long after they have forgotten price. The most successful companies on earth are those that manage to give top quality at a reasonable price.

Our country proved to the world that it could be done. Every businessperson must ask himself or herself, "How is my customer's life somehow improved, upgraded, bettered because they used my product or service? What is my contribution to society beyond that of earning a living?" Similarly, a father and mother should ask themselves, "What are we contributing to our children besides food, clothing, school, and shelter?" It is this greater purpose that spells the difference between that which is average and that which is great, and none of us can ask that question of ourselves too often.

A CONSCIOUSNESS OF COMPETENCE

The greatest man is he who chooses right
with the most invincible resolution.

—Lucius Annaeus Seneca

One night a few years ago, I was among a group listening to records. We especially admired a collection of great traditional songs by a man who has been a star in show business for almost a quarter of a century. Someone said, "That guy's really got it." This triggered a discussion on just what "it" is and why so few have it while so many do not. What makes a star, not just in show business, but in any field of endeavor?

The man we were listening to was singing the same songs we had all heard hundreds of times. He was singing the same notes, the same words. Why did he have such a marked effect upon us? What was it about him, as a performer, that made such a difference? As you think about these questions, apply them to a great golfer who is consistently in the top money, or a great ball player, or salesperson, or business-person, or plumber, or doctor, or homemaker. Ask yourself what it is about these people that makes them a little better than those who are just good.

Well, let me give you my opinion on the matter. To begin, all of these stars are in work that comes close to perfectly matching their natural talents; they are not just round pegs in round holes; rather, they are uniquely shaped pegs that have found perfectly matching, uniquely shaped holes. They take to what they do like a duck takes to water. When they are doing that at which they excel, they are in their element and are happier there than any place else. They would be doing what they are doing, no matter how much or how little money they made. To discover whether or not you are in the right line, you need only ask yourself if the same is true of you.

Next, they are wholly dedicated to what they do. Everything else takes second place in their lives. They spend more time, more care, more practice, more thought, more observation upon what they do than do those who are just good...or even very good. I guess you could sum this up by saying they work harder at their specialty than at anything else.

Finally—and it is here that one of the elusive qualities of real greatness makes its appearance—they know they are good, have supreme confidence in themselves, and, as a result, develop what I call "a consciousness of competence." This is what causes them to relax to the degree necessary for true greatness in anything. While others are nervously straining to excel, forcing themselves and in this forcing falling short, the stars are relaxed in the knowledge of their own greatness. The great painter paints boldly, and the great writer writes the same way; there's no hedging, playing it safe, or keeping open an escape route. They burn their bridges behind them in the sure knowledge of victory. They don't always win, but over the years this attitude keeps them in the elite ranks of stardom.

FAILURE CAN BE GOOD

Success does not consist in never making mistakes
but in never making the same one a second time.

—Bernard Shaw

H as life ever shown you that the right to fail is as important as the right to succeed? If we didn't have bad weather, we would never appreciate sunny days. One hardly ever values his good health until he becomes ill. And I have never known a successful man or woman whose success did not hinge on some failure or another.

There is an old saying that goes, "It is impossible to succeed without suffering. If you are successful and have not suffered, someone has suffered for you; and if you are suffering without succeeding, it is so that someone may succeed after you. But there is no success without suffering."

Success in the world—any kind of success—is like a universal college degree. It can be earned only by following a certain course of action for a definite period of time. It is impossible for real success to be easy. Success also follows a kind of natural selection. Only those individuals who are willing to try again after their failures, those who refuse to let defeat keep them down for long, those who seem to have some strange inner knowledge that success can be theirs if they just stay with it long enough, finally win their diploma in life.

Most men and women who have earned success will tell you that often, just as they felt they were finally reaching the point in life on which they had set their hearts, the rug was pulled out from under them and they found themselves back at the starting line again—and not just once or twice, but many times. Thus, only those of patient persistence are rewarded. But those who do not achieve great success in life are by no means failures. They are successful in their way because they have what they really want. They simply did not want great success enough. They're happy with what they've got, and there is nothing wrong with that.

One day, a young man came to my office and told me he wanted very much to make a great success of himself. He asked if I could show him the secret. I told him to decide definitely upon what he considered success to be for him and then work at it for 12 to 16 hours a day until he had achieved it; and when he wasn't working at it, to think about it. By doing this, he could reach his goal in perhaps five years or so. However, to achieve success, he must force himself back on the track every time he strayed off, realizing that failures are as necessary to success as an excavation is to a basement. I never saw that young man again. I wonder if he took my advice.

Successful people are dreamers who have found a dream too exciting, too important, to remain in the realm of fantasy. Day by day, hour by hour, they toil in the service of their dream until they can see it with their eyes and touch it with their hands.

BIG BUSINESS
STARTED SMALL

A wise man will make more opportunities than he finds.

—Francis Bacon

These days we hear a lot about big business and how much bigger it is getting. But there is nothing wrong with expansion, and one of the most interesting things about it is that every business, no matter how big it might be today, started small. One of the largest corporations in the United States was started with only a few thousand dollars of borrowed money, and after ten years of operation had only $6,000 to its credit. And another good thing to remember is that every business, no matter how big or far flung, no matter how many thousands of employees or how many skyscraper office buildings it may have, got its start in the mind of one human being.

Committees have their place when it comes to considering and solving problems. But every good idea had to start in the mind of one human being and usually came as the result of something he observed. You could start a business of your own this year that in 20 or 30 years could be a growing, far-flung industrial empire, too. People who will tell you all the good businesses are taken or that there are no more opportunities are wrong. Six words lie at the root of any business success: *Find a need and fill it!* The extent of your success will be determined by the need's importance and your ability to fill that need.

Whenever you see a business that is thriving and successful, you may be sure it is filling a need. If it were not, it would just stop and close up shop. The size of a business is controlled only by the number of people it serves and the extent of the need it fills.

I know a man who found his success running a gas station. One day, he was watching a customer and noticed that while the man's car was being serviced he had nothing to do but stand around and wait. He had money to spend, and there were undoubtedly things he would like to buy, things he needed if he could only see them. So my friend started adding these things. He kept right on adding them until now he has built a big sporting goods store alongside his now large and modern gas station. While your car is being serviced at his station, you can buy anything from a package of gum to a boat and trailer. My friend's business was no different from any other gas station in the country until he saw a need and filled it. He could sell it today for half a million dollars. The fact is that there is more opportunity today— far more—than there ever was before. We just have to be able to see it.

HOW'S YOUR CONVERSATION?

*A man of sense and education should meet a suitable
companion in a wife. It is a miserable thing when the conversation
can only be such as to whether the mutton should be boiled
or roasted, and probably a dispute about that.*

—Samuel Johnson

The experts claim that one of the most serious problems of marriage and one of the prime causes for its failure is the inability or reluctance on the part of husbands and wives to talk to each other. It seems the longer two people live together, the more they tend to take one another for granted. It's like driving a brand-new car: at first it's exciting and interesting, but with time, well, it's just a car. People are not machines, and this kind of attitude toward a wife or husband is deadly to a happy marriage. A couple with such an attitude might put on the appearance of marriage, but it is only a matter of contract and convenience.

If there is anyone on earth to whom you can talk, and with enjoyment, it should be the person you have married. The problem seems to come from "letting down." Home becomes a kind of cave where a person feels he doesn't have to behave himself; he can just let go completely. This may be all right for the person living alone, but it never works when two people are living together.

For an intelligent, considerate person, the home should be as important as the office. If an individual does their best all day to be courteous and cheerful in order to get along with their co-workers, why should they feel that they don't have to make the same effort at home? A husband or wife is so much more important than the people at the office that we should go out of our way to be charming, interesting, and cheerful with our spouses.

Now we come back to this business of conversation, the point on which the experts say so many marriages break down. Upon returning home from work, people generally don't want to be confronted with problems and complaints. Instead of unloading their problems on each other the minute they return home, husbands and wives should stick to cheerful subjects. They can talk about the news, a magazine story, or what happened during the day.

Surprisingly, even people who understand the importance of good conversation sometimes fail to recognize its place in the home. Husbands and wives should have more to talk about than any two people on earth. And all it takes is a little effort and an awareness of just how important it is.

SEVEN BLOCKS OF FOG

Worry is interest paid on trouble before it comes due.
—William Ralph Inge

As two young recruits in basic training were talking about expected orders, one confessed that he was worried sick about the possibility of being shipped overseas. The other recruit, an amateur philosopher, said to him, "There's no sense in worrying about it."

His friend asked, "How do you figure that?"

"It's this way," said the philosopher. "There's a 50–50 chance you won't go overseas. If you don't, you've nothing to worry about. If you do, there's a 50–50 chance you won't see action. If you don't, you've nothing to worry about. If you do, there's a 50–50 chance you won't get shot. If you don't, there's nothing to worry about. If you do, there's a 50–50 chance you won't be killed. If not, no worries. If you are killed, you won't have any more worries. So why worry in the first place?"

I don't know if this appeased the worried soldier, but it represents a sound attitude. And if you will reduce the things you worry about to the size they deserve, your worries may well approach the vanishing point.

I remember reading that a dense fog blanketing seven city blocks to a depth of 100 feet could be put in a single water glass. Worry is a lot like that. Worry is a fog that can cloud our vision, knock our perspective off-kilter, and slow us down to a shuffling, halting walk. But like fog, if most of our worries were reduced to their real size, they could all be placed in a water glass.

Experts have estimated that of all the things we worry about, 40 percent will never happen; 30 percent are past, and all the worry in the world cannot change them; 12 percent are needless worries about our health; 10 percent are petty, miscellaneous worries, leaving 8 percent for things that legitimately deserve our concern and thought. This means that 92 percent of the things you worry about, if you tend to be something of a worrier, will never happen. They are either in the past or do not deserve your attention.

The trick is to winnow the 8 percent from the 100 percent. And I suppose this is where being well adjusted, or at least better adjusted, helps. It might be of some comfort to learn that as we get older, one of the really great compensations is that we tend to worry less. Gradually, through the years, we learn for ourselves what the experts try to tell us: that just about all of our concerns solve themselves one way or another or disappear before they get to us. Looking at our worries en masse makes them seem impenetrable. It's like looking at a large crowd of people we must pass through. When we enter the crowd, however, we find we need only pass by one person at a time and that soon we are out on the other side.

Telling someone not to worry is ridiculous. But if you tell them the story of the fog, or that only 8 percent of their worries really deserve their thought and attention, you can usually help them toward a more realistic perspective.

LOSE IT, AND YOU'RE FINISHED!

Every great and commanding movement in the annals of the world is the triumph of enthusiasm. Nothing great was ever achieved without it.

—Ralph Waldo Emerson

About the worst thing that can happen to a human being is to lose his enthusiasm, his excitement, his zest for living.

It has long been a belief of mine that the person who maintains an air of somber boredom, that know-it-all, there's-nothing-new-under-the-sun attitude, is a person with deep and serious feelings of personal inadequacy.

Enthusiasm can be so easily lost. In trying to imitate their elders, which is a serious mistake made by virtually all children (it should be the other way around most of the time), young people often adopt a pose and an expression that seems to say, "Nothing can surprise, charm, or interest me in the slightest." Hands in pockets, leaning against a wall, head tilted slightly back, and viewing an uninteresting world through half-closed eyes, the teenager believes he is the image of the experienced, sophisticated man-of-the-world whose most pressing problem is stifling a yawn.

It would not come as a complete surprise to me if most of this is caused by the tendency of the average adult to try to give the impression to his children that he knows everything in the world worth knowing. How many times has a youngster run with an eager, excited face to his father or mother with some new fact, only to have it waved off with a comment such as, "Yes, yes, I know all about that" or "Are you just discovering that?" Ego-pricking can go a long way toward emptying a child's tank of enthusiasm. So, maybe he makes the mistake of trying to grow up to be like his mother or father. Maybe he is too young to realize that if they are living dull, uninteresting lives, it is because they have permitted themselves to become dull, uninteresting people.

But those individuals who keep their enthusiasm go through life with their wonder, excitement, and interest at a consistently high level. As parents, they are quick to admit to their children that they do not know very much about anything yet and neither does anybody else. They understand the vital importance of fostering and feeding the enthusiasm of youth; they teach their youngsters that the so-called "know-it-alls" are to be pitied or laughed at, but seldom listened to.

The pity of it is that our enthusiasm never dies a natural death. We murder enthusiasm through slow strangulation by imitating the dull, uninteresting people who already have strangled their own natural enthusiasm.

It is a sad day when the curiosity, excitement, and zest for living go out of one's life. There is so much in the world to see and know about; there is so much to do, so much to give, that the loss of enthusiasm for living can only come from a kind of mental blindness. I, for one, hope to keep my enthusiasm—and myself—alive. Whenever you see a person affecting an attitude of bored sophistication, you can rest assured that the attitude is phony and the person has a lot of "growing younger" to do.

THE SECRET OF HAPPINESS

You give but little when you give of your possessions.
It is when you give of yourself that you truly give.

—Kahlil Gibran

Every now and then something is said that affects you like an itch in a place where you cannot scratch. One such remark that I would like to pass along to you here I heard in California while attending the funeral of someone who was very close to me. As I stood on the rolling California foothills in the shade of a row of tall eucalyptus trees, I heard these words: "Fear not that your life shall come to an end but rather that it shall never have a beginning."

The woman whose death had brought me to California had had a beginning in life. She had also accomplished a great deal and was loved by all who knew her. In fact, it was recalling her life that made me think of others whose lives contrasted so sharply—of people who lived solely for themselves. Since their "what's-in-it-for-me" attitude had never sown a single seed, they reaped a barren harvest of their lives.

These are the world's most unfortunate people. That they don't give themselves to others hurts very few, but the unhappiness they bring to themselves is great. We will all know sorrow from time to time, as I did that day in California, but sorrow is one thing; unhappiness is something else.

Running the risk of oversimplifying, I think it can be said that a person is unhappy to the extent that he fails to give of himself to others. This puts happiness, well-being, and peace of mind within the reach of everyone. They can be found in the simplest dwelling or the greatest mansion. They will be found wherever there is a person who has discovered for himself either through long contemplation or through the good fortune of being raised in a happy family, that to get, we must give.

If we give with no thought of getting, there is no limit to the abundance that will accrue to us. We limit our happiness to the extent that we try to measure out happiness to others. Few of us, of course, are real experts in this. It is the most natural thing in the world, it seems, to ask ourselves, "Now just what am I going to get out of this?" Is it hard for us to realize that it is not what we get, but rather what we enjoy, that makes life interesting and fulfilling.

The little lady whose body was in the flower-draped casket that afternoon in California had known this all her life. Her life had been filled with laughter and good cheer all the 69 years, 3 months, and 22 days of her lifetime. What a wonderful way to live! And what a wonderful legacy to leave to those who knew her and who knew the secret of her happiness. Whenever we think only of ourselves, it's like drawing blinds to shut out the sunlight.

DO THEM A FAVOR

Life is to be fortified by many friendships.
To love and be loved is the greatest
happiness of existence.

—Sydney Smith

A good friend of mine came up with an interesting comment the other day. He had recently taken a business problem to a friend in a different business and had asked for help in working it out. He then told his friend that he was doing him a favor by pushing his problem upon him and that he would be happy to have the favor returned by helping with any business problems his friend might have in the future.

I had never thought about doing someone a favor by giving him one of my problems, but the more you think about it, the truer this becomes. There are several good reasons.

1. If he is really a friend, he is glad to help you with your problems. He welcomes the opportunity.

2. By giving him your problem, you are forcing him to think, which is the highest function of a human being.

3. You are making him think along lines with which he is probably not familiar, which stretches his mind and develops his creativity.

4. You make him realize you consider his opinions of value, and this cannot help but make him feel important.

5. By helping you with a solution to your problem, he just might come up with some excellent ideas regarding his own life and business.

I remember reading about Benjamin Franklin having a rather powerful enemy in Philadelphia. For some reason, this person didn't like Dr. Franklin and made no bones about it. In trying to come up with a way of turning this enemy into a friend, Dr. Franklin hit on the idea of asking him to lend a particular book he knew him to have. He found that the man was happy to do so, and with this break in the cold war that had existed between them, they soon became the best of friends. Asking for help is the best way to make the person who is asked feel important, needed, and respected. It is a fact that you are actually doing them a favor.

A man named Robert Hall once wrote: "A friend should be one in whose understanding and virtue we can equally confide, and whose opinion we can value at once for its justness and its sincerity. He who has made the acquisition of a judicious and sympathizing friend may have said to have doubled his mental resources."

William Penn wrote: "A true friend unbosoms freely, advises justly, assists readily, adventures boldly, takes all patiently, defends courageously, and continues a friend unchangeably."

You can say that a true and loyal friendship is an exceedingly rare and wonderful thing. Like a happy marriage or a successful partnership, it needs attention, care, and guarding, and above all, it needs to be needed.

OBEY THAT IMPULSE

*To improve the golden moment of opportunity, and catch
the good that is within our reach, is the great art of life.*

—Samuel Johnson

Refusing to obey our impulses often keeps us from having a lot of fun and perhaps from doing a lot of things we should be doing.

Have you noticed that from time to time, for no particular reason, you will get a sudden impulse—feel a sudden urge? Everything about the idea seems good at the moment; you can't find a thing wrong with it. But instead of acting on the impulse right then, you wait; you sit back and begin thinking about it critically. Pretty soon you can find a lot of reasons for not doing it, or it just passes, and an opportunity is gone forever.

These sudden impulses often come straight out of our subconscious minds, giving us valuable direction—direction we should be taking. By vetoing them, we miss all kinds of opportunities. Dr. William Moulton Marston, a consulting psychologist, says that most people stifle enough good impulses during the course of a day to change the current of their lives. These inner flashes light up their minds for an instant and set them all aglow with the stimulation of the thing. But then they lapse back into the old routine, apparently content to bask in the afterglow that the impulse has provided and content to feel that maybe later on they might do something about it. On this very subject, William James said, "Every time a resolve or fine glow of feeling evaporates without bearing fruit, it is worse than a chance lost; it works to hinder future emotions from taking the normal path of discharge."

At one point in his career, Dr. Marston was employed by a Hollywood motion picture studio, where he worked with Walter B. Pitkin. One day, they were presented with an ambitious production idea from a young promoter. The plan appealed to both of them, but they reacted differently. While Marston was mulling the thing over, Pitkin picked up a telephone and started dictating a lengthy telegram to a friend in Wall Street. The telegram was almost a yard long when it was delivered, but it carried conviction. As a result of Pitkin's spur-of-the-moment impulse, a ten-million-dollar underwriting of a new motion picture was brought about.

Calvin Coolidge remains an enigma to political commentators because the reasons for his actions were seldom apparent and the source of his shrewdness could not be traced. Almost none of our presidents would seem to have been less impulsive than Calvin Coolidge, but the truth is that he literally trained himself to rely on hunches. As a young attorney in a country law firm, he was interviewing a client one day when he received a telephone call and learned that a county political boss was in town. Without hesitation, he cut short his interview and decided to see this man about proposing himself as a candidate for the legislature. The impulse bore fruit and from then on the inner urges of Calvin Coolidge led him consistently from one political success to another.

A sudden impulse to do something you know you ought not to do should be stifled. But when one of those great hunches pops into your mind, act on it right away or you may miss your opportunity forever.

MEMORY IS GOOD— AND BAD

Memory is a capricious and arbitrary creature.
You can never tell what pebbles she will pick up
from the shore of life to keep among her treasures.

—Henry Van Dyke

Everything in nature has two sides: a good and a bad, a positive and a negative. In philosophy, this thought goes back thousands of years to the Chinese Yin and Yang. The Yang is the good, the sunny side of the hill; the Yin is the dark. There is a dualism in everything in the universe. The rain that waters and fertilizes the crops also brings floods; the fire that warms our homes and cooks our meals causes widespread havoc when out of control. We are familiar with the dualism of love and hate.

Have you ever thought about the good and the bad sides of memory? Each of us really has a very short memory. Yes, the subconscious remembers everything, but the conscious mind forgets. We forget our failures, our mistakes, our foolishness, the pain we have caused, the opportunities we have missed, and the love we have failed to give when it was needed. These things pass from our conscious memories as from filters to which they have clung for a while before being washed away by time.

We also forget, unfortunately, the good, and that is bad. We forget the principles, the systems that, if we would but live by them, would result in our achieving the things we seek. We literally forget how to live successfully. If, through some diabolical device, we were constantly reminded of all our past weaknesses and mistakes, we would live in a state of constant depression, fear, and sorrow—a hell on earth. Instead, our conveniently forgetful minds save us from this.

If, through some wonderful agency, we could be constantly reminded only of the good, of those principles and systems that we know work to our benefit and the benefit of society, we would live in a state of optimism, enthusiasm, and hope. We would go from one success to another. It is true that the world's most successful people manage to live in this latter state. They are always aware of what they are doing and where they are going. They know that if they will just do certain things a certain way every day, they will be led to their chosen goals.

Most news seems to be bad. Our newspapers and newscasts are not—and cannot be—filled with all the good that is going on in the world. They report all the news, and the great majority of it seems to be on the negative side: the war, murders, crime, disasters, accidents, swindles, scandals. Furthermore, so many of the people around us, subtly influencing us, are so constituted, or so lacking in the proper education, that they too seem to act and talk on the negative side most of the time. If we live then in accordance with our environment, we too will tend more and more to forget the good and dwell on the bad. This means we will live the major part of our lives on the dark side of the ancient Chinese hill.

What is the solution? It is to find a way to remind ourselves every day, as do the really successful, of those things that lead to success, to good. Otherwise, we will forget the good, along with the bad.

A good airplane pilot carefully follows a checklist before taking off and landing; he does this regardless of his hours in the air. It keeps him successful and alive. You and I need a checklist too, every morning and every night.

IT FILTERS DOWN
FROM THE TOP

The employer generally gets the employees he deserves.
—Sir Walter Gilbey

Have you ever heard the expression "to raise morale"? It's an expression frequently heard in the military service and in organizations of all kinds. But when you stop to think about it a minute, you realize it's a misstatement: morale is not raised from the bottom; it filters down from the top.

The employees of a business—and it makes little difference whether it's the corner supermarket or the largest corporation—will always faithfully reflect the attitude of the person in charge. In the Navy, you'll hear the expression "It's a happy ship." A happy ship is invariably one with a happy skipper.

And strange as it may at first seem, the happiest ship is usually the one that is also the most efficient and performs the best. Good morale is not caused by loose, easy discipline. Frequently, just the reverse is true. A happy skipper is the kind of person who realizes not only the importance of discipline but also the importance of fairness in all things. He is tough when he needs to be tough, but most of all he is competent—knows his business and likes his job. Everybody on the ship admires him for both qualities and will try to emulate him. His crew will knock themselves out to please him and fight hard for him in a tight spot.

In a business firm, people in the lower echelons will never complain of discipline if they know it is fair and if they have a hardworking leader who teaches by example. A relaxing of rules and discipline almost always works in a way opposite to what you might expect; it causes morale to drop. Children also need and want discipline of the kind they know to be fair and logical. Without it, they suffer a loss in personal esteem. Letting children do exactly as they please, when they have neither the maturity nor the wisdom for such responsibility, is unfair and harmful. It results in a kind of juvenile anarchy and a great deal of unhappiness and frustration.

I am not equating employees with children, but the same principle holds true with employees—from the president and vice presidents all the way down to the boy in the mailroom. The president is a kind of company father whose attitude will be reflected throughout the entire organization. This is interesting to know because you can tell what kind of person is at the head of a company by observing the attitudes of the employees. When you see people loafing on the job, it is not a sign of good, but rather of poor, morale. It shows weak and ineffective leadership. If you want to know how good a leader is, don't watch him—watch the people under him. People have a tendency to do no more than is required. The paradox is that the less that is required of them, the unhappier they become.

A person's feeling of worth is closely linked to the way in which they are required to handle their job. The type of people who are natural leaders are the ones who require the best of themselves.

HOW TO STAY HEALTHY

*The belief that youth is the happiest time of life
is founded on fallacy. The happiest person is the person
who thinks the most interesting thoughts.*

—William Lyon Phelps

Søren Kierkegaard, a Danish philosopher, once stated that despair means not being oneself. He pointed out that nothing can make a person sick sooner than feeling useless, unwanted, unchallenged, and unneeded, or feeling that the values other men pursue are empty and joyless for him. This is what happens to many men who retire from work at 65 and die soon thereafter.

I think we need to point out to people who are secretly bored or unhappy that they can live wonderfully long, productive lives if they will take the trouble to find themselves and what it is they really want. If they can find a purpose, it can fill them with new vitality. It will seem as though they have found the fountain of youth—the way to turn back time and live days filled with interest, excitement, and fulfillment. I have met many people who found excitement and youth all their lives, and I am sure you have too. I remember interviewing the inventor of the bulldozer, Mr. LeTourneau, who built the giant earth-moving machines when everyone said it could not be done. People like him never age. Their minds and interests remain as young and healthy at 80 as they were at 20. They have a high degree of empathy with others. They eat and sleep well. They work, play, and love with gusto, and they have an almost impregnable resistance to illness.

A distinguished researcher, Dr. Sidney M. Jourard of the University of Florida, has said: "In thinking about health, I like to conjure up the image of a family of germs looking for a home in which they might multiply and flourish. If I were the leader of such a group and had the well-being of my family at heart, I would avoid any man like the plague as long as he was productively and enjoyably engaged in living and loving. I would wait until he lost hope, or became discouraged, or became ground down by the requirements of respectable role-playing. At that precise moment, I would invade; his body would then become as fertile a life-space for my breed of germs as a well-manured flower bed is for the geranium or the weed."

This is something to think about. You don't have to build bulldozers to be productively and enjoyably engaged in living and loving, but you do need a powerful purpose, a real reason for getting out of bed in the morning, something toward which you are working. This is why people with settled purposes—people who know who they are and where they are going—actually achieve their goals. There is just no stopping them. They are filled with energy, drive, and purpose, and with too much good health even to slow down. You will find no cynicism in them, no suspicion of others, and no worrying about what other people will think. They are much too busy to fool with such nonsense. Are you one of these people? You can be.

HOW TO SOLVE
A PROBLEM

All problems become smaller if, instead of, indulging them,
you confront them. Touch a thistle timidly, and it pricks you;
grasp it boldly, and its spines crumble.

—William F. Halsey

Have you ever encountered a sentence or paragraph that seemed to jump off the page and hit you right between the eyes? It happens to me all the time. I have made a collection of sentences that have affected me that way, at least long enough to make me do some serious thinking. Here is one I ran across the other day that stopped me. There is nothing particularly unusual about it. Maybe it will not affect you at all, but it did me. It was written by Professor Robert Seashore, chairman of the Department of Psychology at Northwestern University: "The happiest people are not the people without problems; they are the people who know how to solve their problems."

People who seem to spend most of their time hanging onto the short end of the stick will tell you that it is because of their problems. I'm sure successful people have problems, too, but instead of complaining about them, they solve them. I wonder how many millions of people have sat and moped because they have problems they think are standing between them and the things they want. They don't realize that trouble distributes itself without favor all over the world. So it boils down, not to a matter of problems, but of people. And that's what it always comes back to.

There are several ways of trying to solve problems. One is the hectic or panic method. Some people want so frantically to solve their problems that they jump at any apparent escape hole like birds knocking themselves out against a pane of glass. When one hole won't work, they try to find another. Sometimes they do, particularly if the problem is simple, but more often than not, it's actually the long way around. It generally results in a lot of wasted time, a lot of worry, and sleepless nights.

Experts claim that it is possible to learn a definite system of problem-solving that will fit most situations. Instead of jumping from one thing to another, think through each problem and its possible solutions before you do anything about it. There are six steps:

1. Define your problem clearly on paper.

2. List the obstacles standing in the way of your solving it.

3. List people or other idea sources that might help solve your problems.

4. List as many possible courses of action as you can think of, and take your time on this.

5. Try to visualize the results of each course of action.

6. Choose the course of action that seems best to you and then pursue it. Stay with it long enough for it to work or to prove that it can't. If it finally doesn't, choose another.

This is the scientific way to solve problems.

THE FEELING OF INFERIORITY

Every man hath his proper gift of God, one after this manner, and another after that.

—1 Corinthians 7:7

A wise man once wrote: "To be human is to feel inferior." Did you know that there is probably not a human being alive who does not have feelings of inferiority? He may not be born with them, but he soon develops them.

Will Rogers said, "We're all ignorant, only about different things." It is also true that we are all inferior in different ways. The person with a healthy, happy attitude toward his world recognizes his inferiorities as a normal part of being human. The neurotic or unbalanced person hates himself for his inferiorities; he feels that they represent weakness and abnormality when they really do nothing of the kind. The well-adjusted person frankly admires others for their talents and abilities without feeling envious. In fact, he doesn't bring himself into comparison at all. He is happily resigned to the fact that he is not the best-looking, best built, smartest, most talented, fastest, cleverest, funniest, most engaging person on earth. Without even thinking about it, he seems to know that every person is a potpourri of strengths and weaknesses inherited from all his ancestors. No two of them were alike, but each one had a slightly different strong point with the standard collection of weaknesses. None of us had a thing to say about who our parents were, and all the vehemence and prayer in the world is not going to do a thing about them. If we have knobby knees, or big feet, or have to wear glasses, or cannot do complicated mathematical problems in our heads, we still represent that which we have been given. The most intelligent and healthy thing we can do about it is to make best use of what we do have.

The experts say that each of us has deep reservoirs of ability—even genius—that we habitually fail to use. We fail to make use of our own private and individual talents because we are caught up in the absurd and impossible game of trying to be like other people who could no more be like us than we could be like them. We forget that other people feel inferior too.

Since there is no one else on earth just like us, how can we be inferior? We are, each of us, one of a kind, defying rigid comparison by any measuring stick. The next time you are in a room full of people, remember that every one of them feels inferior to some degree in many areas, just as you and I do. Consider your strong points, and join the human race. Above all, concentrate on things that take your mind and your interest away from yourself. If you spend your life trying to match the strong points of others, you are doomed to a life of frustration and despair.

THE MAGIC MARBLE

Those who have the largest hearts have the soundest understandings;
and he is the truest philosopher who can forget himself.

—William Hazlitt

My old friend Fred Smith from Cincinnati told me an interesting story about a friend of his who always holds a marble in his hand whenever he talks with someone. Fred noticed that early in any conversation, the man would reach into his pocket and out would come the marble, which he would hold during the chat. Fred asked him about it, remarking that it reminded him of Captain Queeg's ball bearings in *The Caine Mutiny*.

His friend laughed. "This is my magic marble, Fred. Years ago, I had a hard time getting along with people. I knew a great many people but actually had very few friends. One day, I was talking with one of these friends when I noticed his attention was wandering. I was talking, but he was looking out the window, his thoughts a million miles away.

"Later, I got to thinking about it and made a very embarrassing discovery. I realized that I had been talking about myself, that I always did. Conversations with others were really nothing more than opportunities to talk about what I was doing, what I thought, what I wanted. When others were talking, I wasn't thinking much about what they were saying; I was reloading to tell them all about myself. It dawned on me why I had so few friends. I wasn't being a friend. I wasn't interested in what was happening to others and what they thought at all.

"So, I made up my mind to change. I resolved to become interested in others, to let them do the talking, to steer the conversation back to them and their ideas. It's difficult to break a habit of years, but I found the solution the day I dropped into a five and dime and bought this marble. I call the marble 'Importance,' and I make sure it's always on the side of the other person. I have never had a problem with people since. That little marble has made hundreds of friends for me. It has also taught me to quit thinking about myself all the time. I've found myself becoming genuinely interested in others. When that happens, you make friends in a hurry."

Well, that is the story of the magic marble. When I heard it, it made me think long and soberly about my own conduct in conversations. I asked myself if I had been tossing the ball to the other person or trying to hog the conversation with regard to my own interests. I wasn't sure, so I started making sure.

The thing to remember is that other people are far more interested in themselves than they are in you. You accomplish nothing by talking about yourself, but you accomplish a great deal by showing interest in what the other person is saying and doing. You make him feel that he or she is important in your eyes, and whenever you do this well, you might call it "instant friendship." It works like a charm every time.

IT MAKES
A DIFFERENCE

*Kindness is the golden chain
by which society is bound together.*

—Johann Wolfgang von Goethe

Some time ago, I met a man—let's call him John—who had been an artillery officer in World War II. John began to tell me how his battalion came very close to being overrun during the Battle of the Bulge. He and his men managed to hold their position but were exposed to the cold for such a long time period that John's feet were frozen.

The battalion doctor told John that he should be sent back for hospitalization. But the doctor was afraid that, because of the sudden great surge of injured soldiers flooding back from the front, the rear echelon surgeons might amputate John's feet. The doctor suggested that John stay where he was and, while he could not promise anything, he would try his best to save his feet.

As it turned out, the doctor was able to do just that. Today, the Battle of the Bulge and the frozen feet are only a memory, but a big part of that memory is of a doctor who went to a lot of special trouble despite his crowded, hectic days.

We can all look back to someone who took special pains to help us. In many cases, it was a conscientious parent or teacher who refused to be satisfied with merely doing his or her job and no more. I think there is a lesson here for all of us: what we do is important. We should never get the feeling that what we do is not important and therefore take the easy or expedient way out of a situation.

You can never tell when something you might say or do—just a little extra effort on your part—might go a long way toward helping someone. That person will remember you and your action, or your words, for many years to come. He may even pick up the baton of helpfulness and pass it along to someone else.

You don't have to wait for large and important occasions to be helpful. The opportunity is present every day. Just as we have been helped by thoughtful and conscientious people ourselves, we will do well to remember that a word, an act of kindness or generosity can make a big difference in someone's life. And that someone may be numbered among your children, your friends and associates, your neighbors, or even passing strangers.

Every day of your life is filled with opportunities to be larger instead of smaller, polite and thoughtful instead of rude or careless; to love a little more and hate a little less. By these small acts, you will improve your image in the minds of others. By your actions, you will be demonstrating to the world that you are mature enough to take the initiative in being helpful, rather than just doing the least you can.

As with anything else, the best place to start is where you are right now. Of one thing you can be certain—you will never be sorry for having been kind. It is the times when you are unkind that you will remember with shame. Do not ever say, "What I do doesn't really matter." It does. Wordsworth wrote: "The best portion of a good man's life is his little, nameless, unremembered acts of kindness and of love."

THE CLIMATE FOR GROWTH

*The most agreeable recompense which we can
receive for things which we have done is to
see them known, to have them
applauded with praises which honor us.*

—Molière

One day several years ago, I stopped my car for gas at a service station in Hollywood, California. While the middle-aged owner of the station cheerfully went about taking care of my car's needs, I noticed that although the station was by no means new, it was spotlessly clean. I was particularly amazed by the driveway; it was as clean as if my car were the first to use it. I asked the owner how in the world he managed to keep the driveway spotless with dozens of cars dripping oil and tracking residue from the highways on it. He told me how a common product, sold in every supermarket, was in his estimation the best driveway cleaner in the world. He beamed in response to my comment on the way he kept his place of business. It was a valuable moment for both of us: I learned something of value, and he experienced the pleasure of honest praise.

The need for praise is basic to everyone. With it, people bloom and grow. Without it, they tend to shrink and withdraw into themselves. I remember reading about a woman who left a dozen jars of home-made jelly on the kitchen countertop for several weeks. Finally, she asked her husband to carry them down to the basement. It was only then that he noticed the work she had done and complimented her on it.

We all know children need constant praise and encouragement. When a child brings home artwork that looks for all the world like an unfortunate accident, he still expects an encouraging word. But his need for encouragement is no less than his mother's and father's. Far too many mothers and fathers aren't getting any praise, or at least not nearly enough. Understanding the importance of self-esteem and seeing the never-ending need for reaffirmation of a person's worth, we should make it our business to watch for honest opportunities to give praise—especially to the members of our families and those with whom we work.

There is a subtle but enormously valuable byproduct to this sort of thing: in order to praise others, we need to look for the good. It forces us to concentrate on what's right with people and the things they do, rather than on what's wrong. It focuses our attention on the positive side of the ledger and, as a result, makes us happier, more produc-tive, and more pleasant to be around. Then, too, people like those who praise them and recognize their value. When we give praise, we attract a larger circle of friends.

And finally, giving praise is the best-known way to receive it. It's hard for anyone to compliment a chronic grouch. Whenever you hear someone say, "Nobody appreciates me...nobody gives me credit for all I do," the chances are he is so wrapped up in himself and in getting happiness from others that he has completely forgotten how to give. We should try to find some way to commend those we love every day. Praise, to a human being, represents what sunlight, water, and soil are to a plant: the climate in which he grows best. He does not just want it; he needs it as he needs the air he breathes.

A DAY AT A TIME

*The man who does not work for the love of work,
but only for money is neither likely to make
money nor to find much fun in life.*

—Charles M. Schwab

One of the surprising anachronisms of our age is that the great majority of people still think of success as a matter of luck, getting a break, being born rich, or being crooked. It is not, nor has it ever been, any of these things. The formula for success is known, and it is as simple as adding 2 and 2. But you will have a hard time convincing some people of this—namely, those who still cling to their old wives' tales and who alibi their own failures by perpetuating such nonsense.

Here is the formula for success that will work every time for any man or woman. A lifetime consists of years, months, weeks, and days. The basic unit of a lifetime is a single day. And a single day in our careers is made up of certain acts that each of us must perform. We need only perform successfully each act of a single day to enjoy a successful day. Repeat this each day for a week, and you have a successful week. If you will only do each day the things you know you should do each day and do them as successfully as you possibly can, you can rest assured that you will be successful all the years of your life. You don't have to run around in circles trying to do a great many things. It is not the number of acts you perform but rather the efficacy with which you perform them that counts. Don't try to do tomorrow's or next week's work today. Just do today's as best you can and leave tomorrow's for tomorrow. This is really all there is to it.

The county is full of successful people who don't even know they are successful, and it is also full of unsuccessful people who think they are successful. The important thing is not to slight a single act during the day, because sometimes we do not know how really important some little act may be.

The minute one rises in the morning, he is faced with certain things to do. He should be cheerful, for example, to the other members of his family. A person has the choice of being cheerful or sad. With these two alternatives, no one with any sense or understanding of life would choose to be unhappy.

Then there is our work. Have you ever thought how boring and uneventful life would be without our work? Here again, work consists of a series of things to do. We have only to perform each one as best we can to be successful all day long. Finally, if we can go to bed again in the comforting knowledge that we have done the best we could for that one day, we can know that we are successful. As Emerson put it: "Self-trust is the first secret of success, the belief that if you are here the authorities of the universe put you here, and for cause."

Your job, then, is to play out the role you have undertaken to the best of your ability. Success is nothing more nor less than this. We become dull and bored and uneasy with ourselves and others only when we shirk what we know full well we should be doing. The happiest and most contented people are those who each day perform to the best of their ability.

The truth about success is long overdue. There is nothing mysterious about it. Success can be predicted and measured with mathematical precision and will come to us in the exact degree of the effectiveness with which we live each day.

THE BIG DIFFERENCE

Always hold fast to the present hour.
Every state of duration, every second, is of infinite value.

—Johann Wolfgang von Goethe

One of my favorite stories was told to me some years back by a university professor. While he and his wife were visiting a city in India, he had noticed a Hindu who did nothing but sit by the river. Every time he looked, the man would be sitting there. One day, the professor's curiosity got the better of him and, ostensibly taking a walk, he spoke to the Hindu. To his surprise, the man answered him in excellent English. When asked why he seemed to spend all of his time in such a manner, the Hindu replied that he believed in reincarnation. According to his belief, we have all lived many times before and will live many times again. And then he said, "This life I'm sitting out."

From that extreme to handling a job such as president of the United States, it can be said that what happens to a person during their lifetime is in direct relation to the way they pass their days. To my way of thinking, we should be concerned about two periods of time: the present and the future. Although no one person can be absolutely certain that a future exists for them, they are wise to plan for it.

Some people, it is true, overdo this and concentrate so strongly on the future that they forget to live fully in the present. Millions more, I am sure, are so preoccupied with today or tomorrow that they fail to plan at all beyond the present. Then, of course, there are those who neither plan for the future nor enjoy the present. They are people who seem to lack a consciousness of living. Only a few people spend their time wisely, enjoying each day yet preparing themselves for a pleasant and comfortable future. Are you one of these fortunate few?

I remember a Russian author's story about a young man who was to be executed for murder. As dawn broke, the young man stood at the window of his prison cell, where he could see over the walls to the countryside beyond. It was summer, and, at the first light of the beautiful day, a change came over the young man. Suddenly, he became tremendously interested in seeing the first faint rays of the sun touch the leaves of the trees. He noticed the rich, brown earth and the bright green of the fields. As he gripped the bars of his cell and stared intently at the scene that had played out every morning for countless centuries, tears started down his cheeks. He realized that he was seeing the true glory and the magnificence of the world for the first time in his life.

As the jailers arrived to take him to the place of execution, he was still transfixed by the unspeakable beauty of the sunrise. The wonder of life had been there all along; he had simply waited too long to begin enjoying it. And he was not alone in the world. Since our tomorrows will be unlike our todays, we need to try to visualize them and prepare. But we should be mindful also that life can waste itself while we are preparing to live.

WHO'S THE DELINQUENT?

*In the man whose childhood has known caresses
and kindness, there is always a fibre of memory
that can be touched to gentle issues.*

—George Eliot

Have you ever wondered what goes on in the mind of a juvenile delinquent? Do you really know your children? Do you ever have long talks with your youngsters...listen to their problems, hopes, plans?

I want to share with you a letter that moved me deeply. It was written by a boy with a record as a juvenile delinquent. He wrote it to his parents, who sent it to a Kansas City newspaper with a note reading: "Perhaps, if we share this letter through your newspaper, it will help other parents."

Dear Folks,

Thank you for everything, but I am going to Chicago to try and start some kind of new life.

You asked me why I did those things and why I gave you so much trouble, and the answer is easy for me to give you, but I am wondering if you will understand.

139

Remember when I was about six or seven and I used to want you to just listen to me? I remember all the nice things you gave me for Christmas and my birthday, and I was really happy with the things—about a week—at the time I got the things, but the rest of the time I just wanted all the time for you to listen to me like I was somebody who felt things too, because I remember even when I was young I felt things. But you said you were busy.

Mom, you are a wonderful cook, and you had everything so clean and you were tired so much from doing all those things that made you busy; but, you know something, Mom? I would have liked crackers and peanut butter just as well—if you had only sat down with me awhile during the day and said to me, "Tell me all about it so I can maybe help you understand."

And when Donna came I couldn't understand why everyone made so much fuss because I didn't think it was my fault that her hair is curly and her skin so white and she doesn't have to wear glasses with such thick lenses. Her grades were better, too, weren't they? If Donna ever has children, I hope you will tell her to just pay some attention to the one who doesn't smile very much because that one will really be crying inside, and when she's about to bake six dozen cookies to make sure first that the kids don't want to tell her about a dream or a hope or something, because thoughts are important, too, to small kids, even though they don't have so many words to use when they tell about what they have inside them.

I think that all the kids who are doing so many things that grown-ups are tearing out their hair worrying about are really looking for somebody who will have time to listen a few minutes and who really and truly will treat them as they would a grown-up who might be useful to them. You know— be polite to them. If you folks had ever said, "Pardon me" when you interrupted me, I'd have dropped dead!

If anybody asks you where I am, tell them I've gone looking for somebody with time because I've got a lot of things I want to talk about.

Love to All,

Your Son.

Yes, that's the letter of a boy with a police record.

How about taking the time to talk with your kids, listen to what's bothering them, find out what they think. Let them know they are important to you. Let them know you love them and respect them as persons.

WHEN YOU'RE TIRED

*Vigor is contagious; and whatever makes
us either think or feel strongly adds to
our power and enlarges our field of action.*

—Ralph Waldo Emerson

The next time you get the chance, here is a little survey you can make. On any given morning, ask people how they feel. Particularly, ask secretaries, elevator operators, and others who work for wages, as opposed to homemakers who work but don't get paid for it. Maybe it is different in your town, but in mine the answer you will get about 85 percent of the time is "I'm tired." Have you ever noticed how common this is?

And if the truth were known, it is a lot of nonsense! Do you know that you have deep, hidden reservoirs of power you may never have tapped?

Many years ago, I discovered Professor William James's wonderful little book *On Vital Reserves*. In it, he says that everyone knows what it is to start a piece of work, either intellectual or physical, feeling stale. And everyone knows what it is to warm up to his work. The process of warming up is particularly striking in the phenomenon known as "second wind." Now, usually, most people stop working at the first sign of fatigue. They say, "Boy, I'm bushed," and that's it for the day. As Dr. James put it, "We have then walked, played, or worked enough, so therefore we desist." We simply quit. This sort of fatigue forms a kind of wall inside of which, as a rule, we work and live our lives.

But if an unusual necessity forces us to press onward, a surprising thing occurs. The fatigue gets worse up to a certain critical point; then gradually, or suddenly, it passes away and we are fresher than before. We have evidently tapped a level of new energy that had until then been masked by the "fatigue barrier" we usually obey. In fact, we may have discovered that we have the third and fourth winds. This phenomenon occurs in mental activity as well as physical, and in some cases we may find, beyond the fatigue point, stores of energy that we never dreamed we possessed.

Evidently, we stockpile reserves of energy we don't ordinarily use. And these reserves will only go to work when we demand enough of ourselves. Only a few exceptional persons make any serious demands of themselves. The great majority of us miss the far greater accomplishments of which we are capable—and the greater joy in living this would bring to us—because we quit and sit down, gasping, at the first sign of fatigue. And I think this situation has been getting steadily worse.

I remember one Sunday when I knew I had to write ten radio shows all in one day. I got started at nine o'clock in the morning, and by five o'clock that afternoon I was so bushed that I could hardly think. But I still had five shows to write so I kept at it. All of a sudden, I felt better and had more energy than I had previously, and by 1:30 the next morning when I finally finished, I felt great. Sixteen and one-half hours of steady mental work, and I was fresh as a daisy! But I had felt like quitting after only seven or eight hours! The next time you get tired, keep at it and see what happens.

Each of us has a tremendous second wind, mental and physical. Passing through the fatigue barrier to draw upon our idle reserves can make the difference between existing and really living.

HOW TO GET
WHAT YOU WANT

When a man has not a good reason for doing a thing,
he has one good reason for letting it alone.

—Sir Walter Scott

A very wise man once said, "If you can tell me what you want, I can tell you how to get it." He was a wise man because he knew that the problem with people is not their ability to achieve what they want. The great majority of people who are dissatisfied with their lives, who feel the world is passing them by and that they are not getting anywhere, are not suffering from a lack of ability—far from it. They are suffering from not having decided where they want to go.

William James, the father of American psychology, put it this way: "If you would be rich, you will be rich; if you would be good, you will be good; if you would be learned, you will be learned. Wish, then, for one thing exclusively and not for a hundred other incompatible things just as strongly."

So the secret to achievement is to decide on one thing you want very much. Yes, there are lots of other things you want too, but one thing at a time. Write down all the things you want and then pick the one, just one, that you want more than the rest. Stick with that one thing until it is achieved, then go on to the next item on your agenda. A man following this course can accomplish more in five years than the average man accomplishes in forty. This is because the average man never seems to make the one decision that would give direction and purpose to his life.

A gentleman by the name of Edward Bulwer Lytton put it this way: "The man who seeks one, and but one, thing in life may hope to achieve it; but he who seeks all things wherever he goes, only reaps, from the hopes which he sows, a harvest of barren regrets." This is the whole point. Seek one thing, not two or more...one thing at a time.

The next question: "How do I know I have the ability to achieve what I want?" The answer is that we do not seriously want things we don't have the ability to achieve. We all seem to have a built-in governor that keeps us from wanting things beyond our capabilities. That is why one man sets his heart on becoming a lawyer while another applies for a job with the forest service or in an automobile factory. The wide spectrum of occupations and accomplishments shows us the diversity of human desires. Seeing a man working atop the dizzying heights of the steel skeleton of a skyscraper, you have probably said to yourself, "I wouldn't do that for all the money in the world." But he enjoys the work and will do it for so much an hour.

Have no doubt that you can accomplish your goal. It is deciding on the goal that can be the most crucial decision of your life. It has been written, "Providence has nothing good or high in store for one who does not resolutely aim at something high or good. A purpose is the eternal condition of success."

HOW'S YOUR IMAGINATION?

The faculty of imagination is the great spring of human activity,
and the principal source of human improvement.

—Dugald Stewart

Once upon a time, a man took his girl on a picnic. It was a warm summer day, and they had chosen as the picnic site a small island two miles from shore in a beautiful lake near their home. The man rowed his young ladylove to the island. At this point, she decided that she would like some ice cream, so the young man again climbed into the boat and began the four-mile round trip to shore and back. As the perspiration began to stream down his face and his back and arms started to ache, he pondered two things. The first was why a man permitted himself to be pushed around by a pretty girl. Finding no satisfactory answer to that age-old question, he turned his mind to why it was necessary to row a boat at all. He pictured himself sitting comfortably in the boat with the breeze blowing in his face and with a small motor propelling the boat for him. Later, he developed the outboard motor, married the pretty girl with the craving for ice cream, and earned a fortune—all because a four-mile, solitary row made him think: *Big ships had motors and propellers; why not small boats?*

When the Wright brothers invented the airplane, motors had already been invented; so had gliders. They put the two together and devised the airplane.

How is your creative imagination? Are you a curious observer? Do you ever play the creative game? Take any object; it can be a hairpin, a jackknife, a doorknob, anything at all. Ask yourself if it has to be the way it is. Stare at it; study it. Could it be different? Can it be improved? You don't have to be an inventor. This is just an exercise for improving your creative imagination. It can be applied to anything from raising kids to cooking better meals or making more money.

Training the mind to become more creative is a game any number can play at any time, anywhere. It can put new zest and interest into your work, more fun into your days. At dinner, you can play the game with the whole family taking part; just pick an object and ask, "Why is it that way? How could it be improved?"

THE FIRST LAW OF BUSINESS

No one can become rich without enriching others.
Anyone who adds to prosperity must prosper in turn.

—G. Alexander Orndorff

O*ur rewards in life will always be in direct proportion to our contribution.*

This is the law that stands as the supporting structure of all business and also of our personal well-being. The paradox is that most people either don't know about this wonderful law or think that somehow it applies only to the other guy, the way drivers believe we ought to have speed limits—for other drivers. Well, the one predictable thing about most people is that they are consistently wrong.

For example, let's take this law of our rewards in life being in direct proportion to our contribution. Like many great ideas, it's really nothing more than a paraphrasing of a biblical admonition: "As ye sow, so shall ye reap." But for a moment, look at it this way: laws are good or bad, depending on how we use them. The law of gravity keeps us from flying off into space, but it will also kill us if we step into an elevator shaft. There is nothing wrong with the law of gravity.

If we misuse it, there is something wrong with us. We are either ignorant of the law or just plain stupid.

Now, let's get back to the law of rewards and contributions. It's like an apothecary scale, the kind with a crossarm on top from which two bowls are suspended—a delicate and honest mechanism. Let us label one of the bowls "Rewards" and the other one "Contributions." Right here we encounter the problem. Most people concentrate on the bowl marked "Rewards." That is, they want things such as more money, a better home, college for the kids, travel, and retirement—all rewards. But in this hungering for rewards, they are forgetting the bowl marked "Contributions." In other words, they are concentrating on the wrong bowl. They are like the man who sat in front of the stove and said, "Give me heat, and then I'll give you wood." He could sit there until he froze to death. Stoves don't work that way; neither does life. All we have to do is concentrate on the bowl marked "Contributions"; life and the first law will automatically take care of the rewards! Yet it's a fact that most people have this backward.

But what do we mean by *contribution*—and to whom do we contribute? You can define contribution as the time and effort you devote to whatever it is you do. And your contribution is to mankind, beginning with the people you directly serve. So you can break it all down to a very simple statement: your rewards will be determined by the way you do your job. In our exploding economy, if a person isn't happy with his rewards, he should take a good, long look at his contributions. This may seem a hard, ruthless way of looking at things, but remember that laws like this are neither good nor bad; it depends on what we do about them.

THE 95 PERCENT

To follow foolish precedents, and wink with
both our eyes, is easier than to think.

—William Cowper

If someone asked you, "Do you think you are just like most other people?," you would probably answer, "no." Almost everyone feels he is an unusual individual—different from all others. And it's true; no two human beings are exactly alike. But it's paradoxical that while most people like to think they are different, they try as hard as they can to be alike.

In the past few years, you have probably read and heard a lot about the word *conformity*. People are always telling us to be different, to think for ourselves, to be individuals. But do you know why? Well, let me tell you why I think it is an excellent idea to take a good, long look before you start acting and thinking like everybody else.

It seems, from the earliest beginnings of the human race, there have always been two main groups of people. One group is large; it is estimated to consist of about 95 percent of any society. The other is small—about 5 percent. It's uncanny how populations seem to insist on dividing into these two groups: the large group of followers and the small group of leaders. Apparently, the people in the 95 percent group never get the word, for they seem to make the same mistakes over and over again and always wind up with the short end of the stick.

For example, out of all the young men who start even at age 25, 40 years later—by the time they are 65—only 5 percent are financially independent. The rest miss the boat. And while money is not *everything*, it is an indication of how people handle their lives. Any man, barring a rare catastrophe, can save enough money in a 40-year working career to be financially independent by the time he is 65. But only 5 percent know enough at the beginning to plan and save before it is too late. The others will be heard to say, "I wish I had."

The big question is, Why didn't they? Further, in this country of ours, anyone can get a good education, even if he does not have enough money to go to college. Every town has a public library bursting at the seams with knowledge, perfectly free if you get the books back on time. But do you know how many continue to learn and develop their minds after they get out of school? That's right—about 5 percent! In fact, a well-known educator once said that as far as 95 percent of the people are concerned, all the great books, with their priceless stores of knowledge, could be taken out in a field and burned, and they would never be missed—only the 5 percent would miss them. This leads one to the conclusion that 95 percent of the people have absolutely no interest in acquiring knowledge. High school and college diplomas are fine, but they are only meant to prepare us for a life of learning so that we can continually improve and move on to new and better achievements.

Most people just go along—acting alike, thinking alike, doing the same things. They feel this must be the safe way. The trouble is that the crowd is all wrong. Traditionally, it doesn't know where it is going and, as a result, doesn't get anywhere. If you want to follow in somebody's footsteps, fine—just make sure he or she is worthy of emulation. Your friends down the block just may not know where they're going.

STILL THE BEST RULE

Let everyone regulate his conduct...by the golden rule
of doing to others as in similar circumstances we would have
them do to us, and the path of duty will be clear before him.

—William Wilberforce

During the past hundred years, there have been millions of words written about how to succeed in our personal and business lives. They have told us how to walk, how to smile, how to be enthusiastic. Our magazine, newspaper, radio, and television media tell us how to smell sweet, glow with health, and stay young-looking.

Fine. Each of us wants to sell himself to those who are important to him—his family, his friends, his boss, his co-workers, and his customers. And during many of the past years, I have tried to discover for myself how a person might succeed in life. I have made hundreds of speeches to sales and business groups of all kinds, in just about every state in America. From my talks with top-flight businessmen, I have taken enough notes to fill a good-sized garage, all the while trying to draw a composite picture of the really outstanding, successful person. I have talked to old-timers and very young people, extroverts and introverts. Incidentally, you might be interested to know that a very large percentage of successful people are introverts.

They are miles from being the hearty, bluff, backslapping, hail-fellow-well-met, give-me-that-microphone-I-want-to-say-a-few-words kind of people. Instead, they are just very nice, warm, friendly people, with homes and kids, who decided they wanted more out of life than the average person settles for.

Maybe you will be a little surprised by what my survey uncovered. You might say that I took everything I learned from these people and jammed it into a big wine press, squeezed the whole thing down to its very essence, distilled the essence, and, like Dr. Curie, was left with a radiating substance of incredible power. But as perhaps you already know, this glowing, wonderful thing I found was not new. In fact, it was incredibly old. Like the sun itself, it has been renewing itself all these centuries and is just as bright and warm and life-giving today as it ever was. When I realized what I had discovered, I knew I had seen it somewhere before; so I pulled down an old, dusty book from my office shelf and finally found the passage that puts it into better words than I or anyone else I know ever could.

You can look it up yourself. It is in Matthew 7:12, and it reads: "Therefore all things whatsoever ye would that men should do to you, do ye even so to them: for this is the law and the prophets." Simple, isn't it? It is so simple, as a matter of fact, it is completely overlooked by the great majority of people. It is the simple, common, everyday things we take for granted that we miss seeing. I remember hearing a man on a train once say, as a fly landed on his sleeve: "They call it the ordinary housefly. You think it's ordinary? Try making one sometime." Anyway, that is one of the secrets, if you want to call it a secret, of the world's most successful people. They practice one of the world's oldest and best rules—the Golden Rule.

YOU'RE DIFFERENT

Every human being is intended to have a character of his own;
to be what no others are, and to do what no other can do.

—William Ellery Channing

Have you ever found yourself saying, "I wish I were like such-and-such a person?" When we were kids, it was almost impossible to go to a movie without wishing we were the hero. For a while we lived, in a vicarious way, the dangerous, exciting, or romantic life of make-believe we saw on the screen. But the chances are excellent that we would be completely miserable if it were really possible to trade places with someone else.

One of our most common and worst mistakes is to cover up our own abilities and potentialities by trying to be something we are not. A person could spend a lifetime studying the writings of Hemingway and never be able to write like him. The same would apply to acting, singing, painting, or just about anything else. If the person trying to write like Hemingway would write naturally, he would have a much better chance of succeeding. And even more important, he would develop himself as an individual he is meant to be.

As Dr. Ernest Holmes once wrote, "Deep within us...within you and me and all people...something was planted by Life...something that is trying to come forth into fruitage through human endeavor." But it cannot very well come out if we are trying to be something we are not—if we are conforming to a particular group because we think that is the right, or the fashionable, thing to do. I often wonder, seeing a morning train full of commuters, how many of them are really engrossed in and enriched by what they are doing.

All too often they take on the appearance of a herd of cattle on its way to the slaughterhouse. They seem to be playing a part in a play they don't understand, on a stage that is not necessarily of their own choosing. And since they find no real peace or fulfillment in their work, they do their jobs in a perfunctory manner as quickly and easily as possible so that they can quit in the evening and lose themselves in some convenient escape. This is not living; this is really nothing more than waiting for the whole thing to end. This is play-acting.

Finding the real selves we usually keep buried is like prospecting for gold. It is not necessarily easy, but we don't mind the digging so much when we know the gold is really there. It is not like plowing barren ground; riches are there—sometimes way down deep, but somewhere in all of us. And unless a person can find their true self, they will never really know what it means to be fulfilled—to wake up in the morning eager for the day to begin and to end reluctantly a day that has been filled with interest and challenge and that has taken some of the best they had to give. The most interesting journey a person can make is that of discovering himself.

ANTICIPATING
THE DESIRABLE

No wild enthusiast ever yet could rest,
Till half mankind were like himself possess'd.

—William Cowper

O ne of the more painful aspects of being in business is that from time to time, you wind up at a convention, find yourself in a crowded hall, and hear someone on the platform shouting his lungs out telling you that you have to be enthusiastic. This is as absurd as telling someone he has to be happy or that he should suddenly laugh or cry. I wonder if these people know what enthusiasm really is. Human beings are enthusiastic because something caused them to feel that way. Enthusiasm is an effect, like happiness or sorrow. Each of these conditions is the result of a cause.

I remember how painfully embarrassing it was for me on one occasion when a nonentity who would not let go of the microphone shouted, "All right—everybody stand up!" Right then I started looking for a convenient exit. There wasn't one. Naturally, everybody stood up, and then he said, "Now I want you to shout at the top of your voices, 'Boy, am I enthusiastic!'" This was particularly painful for me because I was among those at the speakers' table. The whole assemblage could see us making fools of ourselves. But we all said it and then sat down quietly, squirming with self-consciousness. If there was one emotion I did not feel, it was enthusiasm. The emotions I felt were helpless rage and embarrassment. I believe a person is enthusiastic because of something he wants and feels he has the ability to bring about. Just as a child is excited about going to the circus, an adult becomes enthusiastic because he or she anticipates a very desirable event or situation.

People become excited to the extent that they realize they can have the things they want and can live the kind of life they want to live. When an individual sees something in a store window, wants it very much, and knows they can buy it, they are enthusiastic about it. If they feel it is completely beyond their ability to obtain, they will not be enthusiastic, just wistful.

People become enthusiastic as they recognize their power to achieve their goals. If they feel they are being exhorted to reach goals that are beyond their capabilities or desires, nothing—not all the arm waving and shouting in the world—is going to enthuse them deeply, motivationally.

A human being becomes enthused when it dawns on them that they have talents and abilities that are uniquely their own and have the capabilities to reach a place in life they determine they would like to reach. Charles Kingsley said, "We act as though comfort and luxury were the chief requirements of life, when all that we need to make us really happy is something to be enthusiastic about." Emerson said, "Every great and commanding movement in the annals of the world is the triumph of enthusiasm."

It is true that nothing great was ever achieved without enthusiasm. But each of us must first find for ourselves the suitable object for this emotion.

HOW TO BE UNHAPPY

Some of the best lessons we ever learn, we learn
from our mistakes and failures. The error of the past
is the wisdom and success of the future.

—Tryon Edwards

I don't know how it affects you, but something that really makes me sad is hearing one human being criticizing another. Whenever I hear a man on the street or in a restaurant criticizing his wife, or a woman calling down her husband, or either one of them giving the same kind of business to a youngster, it distresses me. Perhaps this is because I have always regarded rancorous criticism as a sign of immaturity. A suggestion given with good humor and love is something else, but I think angry harangues should always be avoided! No two people are alike, and because of this no two people can be expected to behave exactly alike. And just because one person holds a certain opinion is no reason another person should think exactly the same way.

Consider, for example, a man and his wife: like everyone else in the world, each of them is a unique individual with strong points and weak points. When one person falls in love with another, it is the total person they love—the total impression or image. If the lover compared each feature with the same feature on every other person, they would find others superior in some, inferior in others. They would find no two exactly alike.

The critic is dismayed when they see that some attribute of the person they love is not as good or beautiful as it may be in another person. They concentrate on what they come to think of as a flaw or mark of inferiority. They forget that no one on earth can be superior to all others in all respects.

That is why real love—well-adjusted and true love—is so wonderful. The total image is so pervasive that the little flaws disappear; they are not noticed, or they are loved because they are flaws. That is why the poor, deluded person looking for the perfect woman or perfect man is looking for something that does not and cannot exist.

I think the person who frequently criticizes others is bound to be unhappy with life and himself. He concentrates on the negative instead of the positive. He doesn't see the sky; he sees the clouds. He doesn't see the miracle of a child; he sees tiny and perfectly natural mistakes. He concentrates on the specks of dust that may be found on any masterpiece and, as a result, goes through life missing the beauty and the wonder of life.

WHAT WOULD YOU TELL YOUR CHILD?

*A man without decision
can never be said to belong to himself.*

—John Foster

If you learned this was your last day to live and you were asked to write a formula for living to leave to your children, what would you write? What would you say to give them a wise and true course to follow for the rest of their lives?

They say the best way to learn something is to teach it. If you will write out that formula for living with the idea of passing it along to others, you may find that this will clarify your own thinking and remind you of a lot of simple but important things you can apply in your own life.

Almost all confusion results from indecision. It results from not deciding on a course of action. The minute we choose not to make a decision about something, we put ourselves in the hands of circumstances or under the control of others who will make a decision. A great American general once said: "Decide; even a wrong decision is better than no decision at all." He meant that if you make a wrong decision, it will usually become apparent, and you can change it. But if you make no decision at all, you will never find out what is right. Another military-type quotation goes like this: "On the beach of hesitation bleach the bones of countless millions who sat down to wait and waiting, died."

So you might want to tell your youngsters to form the habit of making decisions. Most young people in school are not sure what they want to do when they grow up. They will say, "Why should I study this or that subject if I'm not sure it will be useful in the career I might follow?" Well, I think they should make the decision to get as good a general education as possible. General knowledge will help them make their career decision wisely, and when the decision is made, they will be bound to have done something toward qualifying for it. They'll have a sound background on which to build the specialty they choose.

We adults excuse our indecision too. We say, "Why should I knock myself out in the work I'm in when I don't like it and don't intend to spend the rest of my life working at it?" The right decision here is to do the best work of which we are capable, knowing that good work habits are necessary to success in anything and a high rate of activity, thinking, and studying will help us find the job we want a lot more quickly than just sitting back and hoping for something to happen. Also, by taking this sort of attitude, we are building the kind of references we will need to move into the field we like when we find it. Carlyle said, "The block of granite which was an obstacle in the pathway of the weak becomes a stepping-stone in the pathway of the strong." It strikes me that a block of granite is often a decision.

CONCENTRATE ON THE INVISIBLE

*A fine life is a thought conceived in youth
and realized in maturity.*

—Alfred de Vigny

It has been said many times that if you go through life doing what the great majority of the people do not do, you will probably never make a mistake. This is a generalization, and generalizations are always dangerous. But there is a lot of truth in this one.

For example, most people think the visible things in life are more important than the invisible. They couldn't be more wrong. Opportunity is invisible until we do something about it. A person's dream of what he wants one day to become is invisible, yet it is one of the most powerful forces on earth, responsible for all human progress. Love for family and friends is invisible. Faith, belief, courage, patriotism—all are free, all invisible, yet vastly more important than visible things. And greatest of all, perhaps, is hope—again invisible. If you think about it, I believe you'll agree that all valuable things you have acquired are the tangible result of what at one time were hope and faith.

I have in my notebook a quotation, the authorship of which unfortunately I cannot ascribe. It goes like this: "There is a thinking stuff from which all things are made, and which, in its original state, permeates, penetrates, and fills the interspaces of the universe. A thought in this substance produces the very thing imagined by the thought. Man can form things in his thought and, by impressing his thought upon formless substance, can cause the thing he thinks about to be created."

Things are really nothing more than thoughts that have become real. As William James once put it, "If you only care enough for a result, you will most certainly achieve it." So if there is something you want very much, think about it and keep thinking about it. Sooner or later, you will find a means of achieving it. But, be careful! As Emerson has written: "Be very choosy therefore upon what you set your heart. For if you want it strongly enough, you'll get it."

A surgeon entering the operating room is only living in reality what was once a dream in his mind. The same is true of all of us, from the young wife and mother, to the astronaut, to the man who finally gets his golf handicap down to ten. Hope, a strongly held thought, is nothing more than the invisible picture of what will one day be reality.

To quote Leigh Hunt: "There are two worlds: the world that we can measure with line and rule, and the world we feel with our hearts and imagination."

THE WORLD
WE LOOK FOR

I find the great thing in this world is not so much where
we stand, as in what direction we are moving.

—Oliver Wendell Homes

Among the writings of Henry David Thoreau I came across this statement: "Many an object is not seen, though it falls within the range of our visual ray, because it does not come within the range of our intellectual ray"—in other words, because we are not looking for it—"So, in the largest sense, we find only the world we look for."

Show two people the same picture, and each will see a different scene; each will extract from what he sees that which he happens to be predisposed to look for. Different people looking out of a train window as they pass through the outskirts of a city will see the same thing from entirely different viewpoints. One will see a depressing, rundown neighborhood. Another will see an ideal plant site. Still another might see a marvelous opportunity for a real estate development. The passing scene might give someone else an idea for a story, or a poem, or a song. Another, his face buried in a magazine, will see nothing.

The world presents to each of us every day that which we seek. There is not a neighborhood or area that does not offer abundant opportunity to every person living there. That opportunity is limited only by the viewpoint of the inhabitant.

Some years ago, a Wisconsin farmer was stricken with polio and left paralyzed. Flat on his back, unable to farm his land, he was forced to push back his intellectual horizon; he was forced to think creatively, to take mental inventory of his assets and liabilities. Without moving from his bed, he built one of the country's largest and most successful meatpacking companies. Unable to use his hands and feet, he was forced to use his more priceless possession—his mind—and he found it contained all the riches he and his family would ever need. Where before there was only a farm, now there are great industrial plants employing thousands. I am sure that when his friends and neighbors learned of his affliction, they wondered how he would manage to operate his farm and care for his family. He simply looked at the farm with new eyes; he saw what he had failed to see before, even though nothing had changed, except his own mobility.

Every one of us lives in a kind of iron lung of his own fashioning. Each one of us has opportunities just as great as that Wisconsin farmer's. But few of us are forced to reach so far into the deep reservoirs of ability within us, and fewer still know the joy and excitement and never-ending interest that can be found in our daily lives when we learn to look at our world as Thoreau looked at his. Surrounded by miracles and limitless opportunity, some people manage to find only boredom and insecurity. As Thoreau said, "We find only the world we look for."

THEY'RE NICER AT THE TOP

Mind is the Master power that moulds and makes,
And Man is Mind, and evermore he takes
The tool of Thought, and, shaping what he wills,
Brings forth a thousand joys, a thousand ills:—
He thinks in secret, and it comes to pass:
Environment is but his looking-glass.

—James Allen

Have you ever noticed that the more successful and important people are, the nicer they tend to be? It is all a matter of attitude. You can learn a great deal about a person by studying his attitude. People seem to expect in others the weaknesses and strengths they themselves possess. Consequently, the more confident a person is of his own value as a person, the better his attitude is toward the world in general.

Big people just naturally treat others well. They are smiling, courteous, and confident. Being happy with themselves, they reflect it; they have nothing to fear. But little people often treat others badly, for they themselves have never really grown up or matured. Something has stunted their inner growth, their confidence in themselves, and since they are not happy within themselves, not confident in their own ability and worth as individuals, they can see in the world only their own reflection. As a result, their treatment of others is a kind of punishment of themselves.

By carefully observing how people—particularly strangers—treat you, you can make a fairly good evaluation of what they think of themselves. The employees with the best attitude naturally rise to the top of any business. So the higher you go in any organization, the nicer the people seem to be. Their good attitudes are not the result of their better jobs; their better jobs are a result of their attitudes. Meeting a successful, happy person, people frequently make the mistake of saying, "I'd be happy too if I had what she's got." It's perhaps natural to think her attitude is the result of her success, but just the reverse is true.

William James wrote: "The greatest discovery of my generation is that people can alter their lives by altering their attitudes of mind." All of us attract the kind of life that we, as individuals, represent. That is, before we can achieve something, we must become the kind of person to which this "something" would naturally belong.

If you can visualize how you would act if you had everything you wanted, begin to act that way now and make that kind of attitude a habit. The attitude must precede the accomplishment. Most people have this backward and, as a result, wonder why they never quite make the grade. If you want to be happy, act like a happy person. One day you will wake up to find happiness has come to you, and you will never quite know when the acting stopped and the reality began. That is why Lincoln's comment that people are about as happy as they make up their minds to be is true. As a great teacher once said, "A good mental attitude is even better than mental ability." Your attitude tells the world what you expect from life, and you will receive exactly that—no more, no less.

TEMPER, TEMPER

Self-reverence, self-knowledge, self-control;
these three alone lead life to sovereign power.
—Alfred Lord Tennyson

Of all the creatures on earth, man is among the youngest. It really has not been a very long time since we were primitive savages. And although we are now able to annihilate each other with atomic weapons rather than stone axes, most of us still have difficulty maintaining a calm, smooth, civilized disposition in some of the circumstances that confront us.

Yet the highest type of human being is the one who manages to control the more antisocial of his primitive urges. Take anger, for example. There is no one more disliked or more to be pitied than the person who cannot control his temper. I know, because for years I had the problem. I paid for it, too, in many ways—and it is not worth it!

A mother with staring eyes, flushed face, and clawing hands, screaming in anger at her child, is a ghastly sight. And there's a sad correlation here: the wider she opens her mouth to shout in anger, the narrower is her intelligence. Men who go through life making their families and friends walk on eggs for fear of their infamous and insane rages are small men, really. They have never matured. And being proud of a hot and violent temper is about as intelligent as being proud of dishonesty or stupidity.

Young ladies who smile and warn their young men that they have a quick temper are saying that they are immature and that they will make embarrassing and unsatisfactory wives—and miserable mothers. And millions of them go on to do just that.

The bad-tempered bully, whether in school or in later life, is universally despised. More than that, he is sick. He is proclaiming ignorantly to the world that he has never grown up and that if everything does not go his way, he will turn back the clock of human progress and act like a prehistoric savage with no more intelligence than an ululating gibbon.

As James Allen wrote: "The strong, calm man is always loved and revered. He is like a shade-giving tree in a thirsty land or a sheltering rock in a storm." The same is true of a woman who is well developed enough emotionally to radiate the calming influence of a peaceful mind and heart. These people see through the effects to the causes of things. Instead of screaming at their children, which does no good at all, they take a more intelligent approach. They do not expect children to act like grown-ups. If another adult does something they do not like, they understand why: they will more than likely feel sorry for the person rather than angry.

I cannot imagine anyone wanting to be feared rather than loved. We love people who have developed mature tranquility, and we like to be around them. They have the capacity for indignation, and they are most effective in changing a situation that they know is wrong. In fact, if you are looking for a fight and want to pick on somebody, steer clear of the calm, self-possessed individual. He will make you look like a blithering idiot. And if you would grow into a person people love and respect, develop a calm attitude and a tranquil heart.

WE NEED TO BE NEEDED

*The confidence which we have in ourselves
gives birth to much of that which we have in others.*

—François de La Rochefoucauld

Every man, woman, and child wants security, but only a small and fortunate few ever attain it.

We know, for example, that a job does not in itself offer security. We often find two men working for the same company and in the same department: one of the men is secure in his job, and the other is not. And this is true of people in almost any situation, including the players on the high school football team or the members of a family.

Let me give you one of my ideas about security and see if you agree: I think the people who have the greatest security are those who are doing the most to secure the situation in which they find themselves.

The security of a person working for a company depends upon the security of the company itself. Therefore, those individuals who make the greatest contribution to the continuing success of the company are the most secure; those who do the least are least secure. The boy who contributes most to the success of his football team has the best chance of getting in and staying in the game. So we can say, then, that a person is secure to the extent that he is needed. And he will be needed to the extent that he has developed the capability of doing successfully the things that need to be done.

The areas in which he should develop himself most are those in which he is most depended upon. Most of us accept the fact that we must remain insecure in all but a few situations. I would feel insecure in a professional golf or bridge tournament. I enjoy playing both games for fun and relaxation, but I don't have the skills and experience to compete with the professionals in those fields. And I cannot fly a passenger jet, or command a ship at sea, or even fix my car if it stops running. But we can all develop the security we need for the situations we are regularly called upon to meet and have freely chosen. We can do it by learning to do what we do as well as it can possibly be done. We may not achieve this ideal, but in striving toward it, we will become secure as persons.

Security, then, lies not outside us, but inside. The wonderful thing about developing this kind of security is that we take it with us wherever we go and can never lose it. And like everything good in life, it is there to be earned if we seriously want it.

OH NO, YOU WOULDN'T!

People do not lack strength; they lack will.

—Victor Hugo

A fine woman pianist once gave a performance for a large group of women. Afterward, over coffee, a woman gushed to the virtuoso, "I'd give anything to play as you do." The woman who had given the concert took a sip of her coffee and fixed the red-faced, slightly perspiring matron with a cold gaze. Then she said, "Oh no, you wouldn't!" A hush fell over the group, coffee cups stopped on their ways to and from saucers, and the perspiring matron squirmed in sudden embarrassment. Looking about her, she repeated, but in a softer voice, her original statement: "I would too give anything to play the piano as you do." The female virtuoso continued to sip her coffee and shake her head. "No, you wouldn't," she repeated. "If you would, you could play as well as I do—possibly better, possibly a little worse. You'd give anything to play as I do except time...except the one thing it takes. You wouldn't sit and practice hour after hour, day after day, year after year." Then she flashed a warm smile, "Please understand," she said, "I'm not criticizing. I'm just telling you that when you say you'd give anything to play as I do, you really don't mean it. You really don't mean it at all."

In the pause that followed, a napkin falling to the rug would have rattled the windows. The women looked at each other and then back at their coffee cups. They realized that this woman had spoken the truth. They would like to have her talent now, fully matured and developed; but as for putting in the 20 years of unremitting toil that went into the fashioning of it—no, that was a different matter. Soon, the light conversation was resumed, and the incident was glossed over, but not forgotten.

People are forever saying, "I'd give anything...," but the fact remains that they don't; they give very little, often nothing, to do the things they say they would give anything to do. Those who envy the star performers in any field should realize that across the entire galaxy of achievement the stars are those who did not idly wish for success. They gave their dedication, their singleness of purpose, their days and nights, weeks, months, and years to an unceasing struggle for greater proficiency. And when the talent they have so painstakingly culti-vated for so long begins to bloom, others, who had the same time, the same opportunity, the same freedom, come up to them and say, "I'd give anything to be able to do what you're doing, to have the things you have." But as the lady pianist said: "I'm just telling you that when you say you'd give anything to play as I do, you really don't mean it. You really don't mean it at all."

Why not become what you dream of? Each of us has the time and the opportunity. If we say we do not, we are perhaps kidding ourselves. With enough effort and perseverance everyone can become great at something. Sometimes it seems there are far too many spectators in the game of life and not enough players. Maybe we are so busy watching the world and everyone else that we forget we have a world of our own to win.

THE LUCKIEST
PEOPLE ON EARTH

*I would maintain that thanks are the
highest form of thought, and that gratitude
is happiness doubled by wonder.*

—G. K. Chesterton

Do you know who the luckiest people on earth are? To my way of thinking, they are those who have developed an almost constant sense of gratitude.

A person who is not conscious of living, of happiness, and of all things living embodies might just as well not be living at all. This is perhaps what Socrates meant when he said the unexamined life is not worth living.

The luckiest people are those who are grateful for their work and grateful that they can do their work and do it well. They are grateful for their children and their wives and husbands. They never take them for granted, never permit them to lose their love, interest, and charm. They are grateful for their lives, their health, their friends, and their opportunities. And they have about them an aura of good cheer and well-being. They are not Pollyannas. They are aware of the ugly and the sordid things that go on about them, but they do not permit themselves to be dismayed. When trouble comes their way, they seem to know that it is only temporary, and they tackle trouble like a linebacker cutting through to nail a quarterback for a ten-yard loss. And when the trouble has been taken care of, they dust off their hands and go charging out into life again.

If I had to pick out the one quality that makes these people different from the millions who live defensive, insecure lives, I would say it is their sense of gratitude. They are so grateful for all the good things that they don't have time for preoccupation with the unpleasant.

Children are experts at this. I once watched a little boy—he must have been about two—at play. Raising himself up quickly, he banged his head on a table. He had hit his head so hard that it made him sit down, and there he sat for a minute, rubbing the spot, with his face puckered up and a couple of big tears in his eyes. Suddenly, though, he got to his feet, and away he went, still rubbing his head but with his mind on more interesting things. There was nothing he could do to alter the fact that he had a new lump on his head, but he was not going to sit in a corner and spend the rest of the day worrying about it.

The grateful people never lose this happy faculty. They expect the best from life and, as we all do, they get what they expect 95 percent of the time. They take their lumps and move out again, looking for things that are more fun and more rewarding. They wake up in the morning grateful that they are alive and go to bed the same way at night. They seem to have an acute consciousness, an awareness that they are living every second of their lives. They enjoy their food and their sleep, their loved ones, and their work.

We all know people like this. And we can learn from them. And perhaps the best way to begin is to develop a sense of gratitude.

NOTHING CAN REPLACE IT

An enterprise, when fairly once begun,
should not be left till all that ought is won.

—William Shakespeare

People often wonder how certain individuals seem to accomplish so much during their lives. Those who achieve unusual success are often regarded as different, geniuses, or lucky, or they are believed to have some magic formula. But the fact is that one thing typifies the successful: persistence.

There is a quotation: "Nothing in the world can take the place of persistence. Talent will not; nothing is more common. Genius will not; unrewarded genius is almost a proverb. Education will not; the world is full of educated derelicts. Persistence and determination alone are omnipotent."

Just as the person who stays with the study of medicine will become a doctor someday, any person who makes up his mind what he wants and has the determination to stay with it will most certainly obtain it. The trouble with most people is that they don't know what they want. They first try one thing and then another, or perhaps they just mark time, waiting for some unknown opportunity to come along. If they would only choose a goal and pursue it with determination and persistence, they could relax in the certain knowledge that although it might take a long time, one day they would assuredly reach it.

Persistence makes dreams come true. If a person persists long enough, he will become qualified for that which he seeks. Talent will help, as will genius and education; the more you have for you, the better. But the fact remains that a person can be quite short in the talent and education departments and still get where they want to go—if only they have chosen their destination.

I have long believed that the reason people do not accomplish more is that they do not know what causes success. They think it is difficult and complicated and involves many years of study, financial backing, and some kind of wizardry. As a result, they do nothing at all. Persistence sounds easy, but it is not easy at all. All kinds of obstacles present themselves, some of them so serious, or seemingly so, that you think there is no way on earth to get around them. At times like these, the person without enough persistence finds it easy to rationalize abandoning his goal. His excuses may sound fine and convincing, even to himself, but they are still excuses—nothing more.

Someone once wrote to me that he had always wanted to write a book but for years had been too busy. Now that he was retired and had plenty of time, he said he was too upset to write. Finding excuses for not doing something is easy; finding the persistence to do it is something else again.

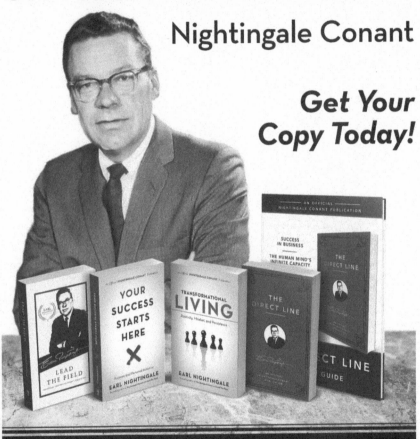